Help Your Children Succeed in High School and Go to College

An Essential Guide for Latino Parents

Mariela Dabbah

SPHINX® PUBLISHING
AN IMPRINT OF SOURCEBOOKS, INC.®
NAPERVILLE, ILLINOIS
www.SphinxLegal.com

Published by: Sphinx® Publishing, An Imprint of Sourcebooks, Inc.®

Naperville Office
P.O. Box 4410
Naperville, Illinois 60567-4410
630-961-3900
Fax: 630-961-2168
www.sourcebooks.com
www.SphinxLegal.com

This publication is designed to provide accurate and authoritative information in regard to the subject matter covered. It is sold with the understanding that the publisher is not engaged in rendering legal, accounting, or other professional service. If legal advice or other expert assistance is required, the services of a competent professional person should be sought.

From a Declaration of Principles Jointly Adopted by a Committee of the American Bar Association and a Committee of Publishers and Associations

This product is not a substitute for legal advice.

Disclaimer required by Texas statutes.

Library of Congress Cataloging-in-Publication Data

Dabbah, Mariela.
  Help your children succeed in high school and go to college / by Mariela Dabbah. — 1st ed.
     p. cm.
  ISBN-13: 978-1-57248-643-0 (pbk. : alk. paper)
  ISBN-10: 1-57248-643-0 (pbk. : alk. paper) 1. Hispanic American children—Education (Secondary)—United States. 2. Education, Secondary—Parent participation—United States. 3. Universities and colleges—United States—Admission. I. Title.

LC2670.4.D33 2007
371.829'68073—dc22
                                                                    2007022729

Printed and bound in the United States of America.
VP — 10 9 8 7 6 5 4 3 2

This book is dedicated to my private cheerleading squad; those friends who are always supporting my next new project…

Silvina Aisenson Lichtmann, Fawzia Afzal-Khan, Gustavo Averbuj, Blanca Aynié, Betina Bensignor, Gilberta Caron, Rosemary Daniele, Claire Dutt, Michelle Flaum, Marisol González, Jerry and Marilyn Hilpert, Isabella Hutchinson, Sandra and Jeffrey Justin, Aitana Kasulín, Rosalind Kennedy-Lewis and Herb Lewis, Steven Kuhn, Susan Landon, Soledad Matteozzi, Alejandro Michell, Ana Mordoh, Mariana Panichelli, Arturo Poiré, Marisela Riveros, George Starks, Karen Tawil, Pachi Veiga, Marjorie Venegas, Ana María and Jorge Villarino and Efraim and Pnina Yuhjtman.

And… to the newer members of the squad:

Cristina Alfaro, Gladys Bernett, Cecilia Gutiérrez, María Fernanda Hubeaut, Lorraine Carbonel Ladish, Alejandro Escalona, Chuck Hurwitz, Gloria Puentes, and Julie Stav.

Acknowledgments

For the most part, writing a book is a lonely undertaking. I get to sit down for hours in front of my computer typing away... So one of the things I like the most about the process is to interview people who are knowledgeable in the subject that I'm covering. For this book, I talked to many parents, students, teachers, school administrators, psychologists, and college admissions officers. Their input was invaluable to me as it helped make this guide very tangible and practical.

I would like to thank everyone who participated in the interview process and especially the following people for the time you took to share your opinions with me:

Fermín Acosta, Jocelyn Acosta, Jorgelina Acosta, Ana C. Ansín, Ricardo Anzaldúa, Anthony Bellettieri, Gladys Bernett, Robin Bikkal, Margaret Boyter-Escalona, Donald Carlisle, Jorge Castellanos, John Cavallo, David Cisneros, Marín Curiel, Alex DeLeón, Katiuska Delgado, Gloria Esteban, Anna García, Eduardo A. García, Warlene Gary, Patricia Garrity, Erick Hamann, Marcela Hoffer, Abe Tomás Hughes, Chioma Isiadinso, Michael Kohlhagen, Martita Mestey, Deidre Miller, Felipe Newlands, Jessica O'Donovan, Stephanie Pagán, Leila Rey, Helen Santiago, María Soldevilla, Charles Strange, Rodolfo Vaupel father, Rodolfo Vaupel junior, Jean Jaque Vel, Marjorie Venegas, and Alfonso Zhicay.

Marjorie Venegas, special thanks to you for reviewing the manuscript and for your invaluable comments!!

Aindree Hamann, my brilliant assistant: you have greatly contributed to making this book what it is.

Michael Bowen, my editor: thanks for the enthusiasm with which you supported the project. Erin Shanahan, thanks for picking up so seamlessly where Mike left off!

Lorraine Carbonel Ladish, thanks for teaming up with me for the Spanish translation. You are the best!

Chuck Hurewitz, thanks for your guidance and complete trust in me!

Contents

Introduction

Teenagers have a way of making you feel that they don't need you anymore. That they are all grown up and independent and that they can take care of themselves. Well, don't let them fool you; they are still children and they need you to support them and help them figure things out. Your support is needed especially during their high school years. However, if you come from a different country, or if you don't have a college degree, you may feel that you don't know how to support your child because you are not acquainted with the American school system.

First, I want you to always remember that supporting your children's education has a lot more to do with your attitude than with knowing specific information. Having ongoing conversations about the importance of going to school, studying hard and going to college is essential. Establishing high standards and holding your children to these standards is fundamental. Making sure you provide the right environment for your children to do their job, which is to study and do well in school, is also a key component for their success. Finding resources for them when you can't help them, paying attention to their changing needs, and most of all being always present are some of the most important things you can do for your children.

I wrote this book to help you understand what high school in the United States is all about so you can better help your children get the best out of it and then go to college. In this country, the higher the degree of education you achieve, the more upper mobility you have, and the more money you can make. It doesn't matter if your family background doesn't include many college graduates or if you don't belong to the economic elite. Your children have the right to go to college, and, with your support, they will.

Below you can see the average annual salary that a person makes according to how much education they have attained.

High school Graduate:	$25,191
Associates Degree:	$31,720
College Degree:	$41,287
Master's (not MBA)	$50,862

Most likely as an immigrant you came to this country to improve your living conditions and to give your children better opportunities than the ones you had back home. The only way to really accomplish this admirable goal is by supporting your children throughout their education. If you came to the United States expecting to stay for a few years and return to your home country and are now here for good, you still want to give your children the best chances to succeed in your adopted country. As you well know, the Latino population is growing rapidly in America. In order for them to assume positions of leadership they will need to be highly educated, and that means completing college and obtaining graduate degrees.

This is a generous country. In this book you will learn how to tap into resources available to your children, like scholarships specifically created to help Latinos and other minorities go to college. I suggest that you learn as much as you can so you can guide your children through these difficult years.

Finally, as you read these pages and acquaint yourself with the educational system in the United States, it is essential that you always give your children a consistent message about the importance of education. Many times, well-intentioned parents don't realize that by not listening to their kids, or by not attending meetings at school, or by not respecting their children's homework space, or by taking them out of school when school is in session, they are sending the message that education is not *that* important. As I said before, supporting your children's education is all about attitude, so you need to make sure that yours is a positive one.

Note for Parents with Undocumented Children

By law, your children can receive education up to the 12th grade regardless of their legal status in this country. This means nobody can ask you or your child for a social security number or for any documents that prove your status. Once they get to college age, the story changes a bit.

Every state has a different policy regarding the right that a public university or college has to ask for a social security number, so you should find out what the situation is in your state. Private colleges can make their own policies, and many times they don't care about a students' immigration status.

Public colleges usually charge a certain fee for residents of the state (*in-state resident tuition*) and a much higher fee for people who are not. Because they are treated as foreign students, undocumented students may get charged the more expensive fee even if they live in the state. California, Illinois, Kansas, New Mexico, New York, Oklahoma, Texas, Utah, and Washington have all passed laws to charge in-state resident tuition to undocumented students who live in the state.

There are scholarships available for undocumented students and private colleges may decide to offer financial aid or grants to anyone they choose. As a matter of fact there was a story in the media recently about a brilliant undocumented Latino student who got admitted to Princeton University with a full financial aid package. Federal financial aid, however, is only available for citizens and legal residents.

Also, as Robin Bikkal, a renowned immigration lawyer, suggests: "Studying helps children preserve their sanity while they wait for possible avenues to acquire lawful status. After high school, they can go to college part time, attend state institutions as in-state residents, or take continuing education courses if that's the only way they can afford school. The parents' job is to keep academically-inclined children in school by helping them continue to study at the post-secondary level and staying within the educational system."

There were two pieces of legislation that in the past were approved by the Senate but stopped by the House of Representatives called the *Development, Relief and Education for Alien Minors (DREAM) Act* and the *Student Adjustment Act* that address the situation faced by young people who were brought to the U.S. years ago as undocumented children but who grew up here and stayed in school and out of trouble. These bills would offer qualified youth conditional legal status and the possibility of a green card. Support for the DREAM Act has grown each year since it was first introduced in Congress in 2001, and many observers believe it has a better chance of enactment this year than it has ever had. To find out more information and updates on this bill visit the National Immigration Law Center's website at **www.nilc.org**.

So, if your child is undocumented, don't despair. John Cavallo, a successful immigration lawyer in New York, says: "Studying makes a difference. The judge wants to know if the kid has been going to school, has been making an effort, has stayed out of trouble. These are all things that influence the case."

The moral of the story is that neither you nor your children should stop the pursuit of educational excellence based on the fact that they are undocumented. Eventually, things get resolved and having a good, solid education under their belts is the best way to guarantee your children's future success.

Chapter 1

Let's Get Some Inspiration

He will never be able to erase the horror of that scene from his soul—of the eight passengers in the truck, five died and two were seriously injured. One of the dead men was his father; another, his uncle. He, Martín Curiel, 18 years old, was unscathed. That only means physically unharmed, though, because the accident— which took place as they returned from picking cherries in Oregon—would profoundly affect his life. He owes his decision to get ahead and do great things to the memory of his father.

Martín's family was made up of Mexican farmers who migrated to California between May and December for the fruit harvest. Martín went to elementary school between the two countries and eventually got tired of waking up at 3:00 a.m. and spending thirteen hours in the fields doing intense and repetitive labor. He realized that the only way he would make more money and improve his situation was to finish high school. That's when he convinced his parents to spend more time in California so he could apply himself and study more.

The night of the accident, Martín, who had applied to college, had asked his father to return a day earlier from the fields so he could attend his college orientation session. "I felt very guilty for what happened and I made myself the promise that my dad would not have died in vain," Martín says. With the help of numerous scholarships he attended California Polytechnic State University, one of California's most prestigious schools of engineering. As his mother only had a third grade education—his father had only been able to sign his name—Martín counted on the parents of a good friend of his to help him navigate the process to obtain scholarships. They reviewed his essays and made suggestions on how to polish them, helping Martín receive about 80% of the grants he applied for.

College was a tough experience for Martín as he was not used to being away from his family. Besides the normal pains of separation, he had to learn to live on his own and do things like laundry and cooking, which he had never done before. He felt out of place, as there were only a few Latinos in school, and he also felt that he was not as well prepared academically as other students.

By his junior year, however, Martín had figured out the system and in the last two years he managed to get his GPA (Grade Point Average) up to 3.9. He graduated with honors at the top of his class. "I realized that to succeed in school you don't need to have money or be smart. With hard work, perseverance and determination you can overcome any obstacle," he explains. "The best thing was that in the end I gained the respect of my engineer friends and I fulfilled my promise to my parents," shares Martín.

Upon graduation, Martín received and accepted a $52,000 offer from Texaco, five times as much money as his entire family was making at the time, and the highest salary ever offered to an engineer from his college. He worked at Texaco for four years and then, encouraged by a mentor, decided to get his MBA from Harvard Business School. He graduated in 2004. "In every rich person's life there was one person at one point or another who broke the cycle of poverty for the family. Through college, Latinos can do that. I am the pioneer. The Curiel family has been poor and ignorant for many centuries. Now that has changed. Now we have lots of opportunities and the chance to give back to the community," says Martín.

And give back he does. He founded *Rising Farmworker Dream Fund* (**www.risingfarmworkers.org**), a foundation whose mission is to use the resources and power of the corporate sector to produce a positive social change in the migrant worker community of the United States. Martin's idea is to facilitate the American Dream of farm workers by giving them access to financial, human, and social capital. He currently works at Deloitte Consulting, one of the largest financial consulting companies in the world making a six figure-salary. He donates 10% of his income to his foundation. Last year he took his mother on a trip to Europe. She is still bragging about it.

Chapter 2

The Basics

If your children were raised in a Latin American country (or if you as a parent were raised there), the prospect of your kids entering high school in America can be a scary one. High schools in this country are usually quite large, and the way they work is quite different from their counterparts in South America. I remember the first time I set foot in a high school in the U.S. I was fifteen and I had come from Argentina to visit my cousin in New York. When the class period ended and all the students came out of their classrooms at the same time and ran through the hallways to their next class, I was terrified. Back home, we stayed in the same classroom throughout the entire school day while the teachers came and went. All this movement felt very strange and chaotic to me. Your children may feel as confused as I was, so I suggest that you offer them all the support they need through this adaptation period.

On a more practical matter, if your children attended school in your home country, and this is the first time they enter the American school system, you need to provide all the transcripts from their old school so they will be placed in the right grade. If you don't bring proof of what subjects (which represent credits here) they have already taken and passed, they may be placed in a lower grade so they can fulfill all the credits required to graduate.

Choosing a High School

Choosing the right high school is extremely important because the right match is one of the essential components on the road to success. If your children attend a school where they feel welcomed, appreciated, encouraged, a school where there is a sense of community and where they feel challenged to give their best and where they feel safe, they will blossom. If, on the other hand, they don't feel comfortable with the adults or with the other kids in the building, if they feel like they don't belong there, if they feel insecure or bored, it is very possible that they will not succeed.

Expert to Parent

Marcela Hoffer, a clinical social worker and mental health coordinator at Columbia University Early Head Start program, suggests that you need to find a school that is *good enough.* "The idea comes from the psychotherapist Donald Winnicott's concept that a mother doesn't need to be perfect; she needs to be good enough. The same applies to a school. You don't need to look for the perfect school but for one that is good enough for your child and that will suit your needs and expectations. If you keep in mind that, at this stage, children will be more interested in pleasing their peers than pleasing you, you will want to make sure you find a school where they have good peers or, following Winnicott's suggestion, *good enough peers.*"

Even though many children attend the public high school of the school district where they live, this is not necessarily the only option. If you live in a large city, you may be able to choose among different high schools within the same school district. If you live in a small town with only one high school and you know that it is not the best option for your child, you may want to consider moving to a different town that offers a better fit. You can also consider a private high school.

The process of choosing a high school is similar to the one for choosing an elementary school. (You may want to read my book *Help your Children Succeed in School, A Special Guide for Latino Parents*, where I talk extensively about that process.) You need to ask a lot of people a lot of questions in order to find the school that best suits your children's needs and future plans. To accomplish this, I suggest that you talk to your local librarian, other parents, teachers, and people from the community.

When you do your research, consider the following issues:

- Is the size of the school appropriate for your children? Is it too big or overcrowded? Would they feel better in a smaller school?

- Does the school have a specialty or does it offer a diverse selection of strands such as technology, performing arts, sports leadership?

- What is the ethnic makeup of the school?

- What percentage of the students graduate every year?

- What percentage of students who graduate goes to college?

■ How does this school rate in violent incidents compared to other schools in the area?

■ Is the school environment friendly and challenging to students?

■ Is there a sense of community?

■ Do teachers have a history of supporting students?

■ What is the teacher to student ratio?

■ What extracurricular activities does the school offer?

It is also a good idea to ask the principal of the school you are visiting: "What kind of student does well in this school?" Your goal is to get as much detailed information as possible to see if your child would do well in that particular environment. Does the school encourage artistic kids, sensitive kids, kinesthetic kids, etc.?

Raising the Academic Bar for Minority Students

Whether you are reading this book while your child is still young and has not yet entered high school, or if your child is already in high school, you will greatly benefit from learning about a number of programs designed to close the achievement gap for minority students.

Many of these programs are geared toward middle school children to help them get into some of the best independent day schools and boarding schools across the country. Others are focused on supporting high school students to enter top colleges and succeed once they are there.

There are many more organizations like the ones I discuss in this section that work at a local level. You should talk to your children's school's guidance counselor or principal about any programs available in your area.

For instance, in New York City there is a very successful program called *Prep for Prep* (**www.prepforprep.org**) that selects 5th and 7th grade students to enter its academically challenging program. These students attend summer courses as well as after school and Saturday classes that prepare them to enter top independent schools.

Let's look at a few national programs that offer wonderful opportunities to help your children succeed academically.

A Better Chance
(**www.abetterchance.org**)
This national organization refers students of color—African American, Latino, Asian American, and Native American—who are at or above grade level and show leadership potential, to around 300 of the finest independent and public schools in the country to be considered for placement and financial aid. You can submit an application if your child has a B average or better and is between the 5th and 10th grades. The students who are successfully placed become part of the *College Preparatory Schools Program* where they receive educational support and leadership opportunities.

Knowledge is Power Program (KIPP)
(**www.kipp.org**)
KIPP is a national network of free, open enrollment, college preparatory public schools in under-resourced communities throughout the country. At these schools

students develop the knowledge, skills and character traits needed to succeed in the best high schools and colleges. It provides a structured learning environment, more time in school—7:30 AM–5:00 PM on weekdays, every other Saturday and three weeks in the summer— and high quality teachers. The program is based on five operating principles: high expectations, choice and commitment, more time, power to lead, and focus on results. KIPP operates 52 schools across the country, most of them middle schools.

Advancement Via Individual Determination (AVID)
(**www.avidonline.org**)
This is a 4th to 12th grade system to prepare B, C, and even D students to be eligible for a four-year college education. Typically these students will be the first in their families to attend college and many are from low income or minority families. AVID pulls them out of unchallenging courses and places them into accelerated tracks. Students also participate in the *AVID Elective Program* for one period a day where they learn organizational and study skills, critical thinking, get academic help from peers and college tutors, and participate in enrichment and motivational activities that make college seem attainable. The program works within schools throughout the country.

The Posse Foundation
(**www.possefoundation.org**)
This national organization identifies, recruits, and trains student leaders from public high schools to form multicultural teams called *Posses*. These teams are then prepared through an intensive pre-collegiate training program to enroll in the top-tier universities nationwide

both to pursue their own academic path and to promote cross-cultural communication on campus. Each posse consists of ten students from diverse backgrounds who are selected for their leadership and academic potential and who are then prepared to attend their chosen college. These groups serve as interconnected support units within an institution and help promote students' individual and collective success. The ultimate goal is to prepare leaders who reflect this country's rich demographic mix.

Remember: There are many programs out there that can give your child the help he or she needs to excel academically. Your responsibility is to become as informed as possible so that you can discuss the options and make informed decisions.

Parent to Parent

Martita Mestey, mother of two daughters, shares: "My youngest daughter wants to go to Penn State and she knows they recruit from a particular boarding school, which costs $35,000 a year. Right now I'm looking for scholarships to pay for it. It's hard for me because I live in Chicago and this particular high school is in Pennsylvania. It makes my stomach hurt every time I think of it, but she knows that if she works hard the university will come and recruit her in high school instead of her going through the application process like her sister did. So, I'm trying to get her into that boarding school."

Keep all your options open before you and your child make a decision about what high school is the best option. Visit **www.schoolmatters.com** and type in your zip code and a one-mile radius around it to get a complete list of public high schools near you. This website provides you with detailed data of each high school including performance in math and reading, ethnic composition, teacher per student ratio, and a lot more. To find the same type of information for private schools, go to **www.petersons.com**. On this website you can also request to receive more information and arrange for school visits.

Inspirational Capsule

Deidre Miller, who has a Master of Science Degree in International Business Systems, was raised by a single professional parent and attended private school K–12. She shares what she got out of going to private school.

"The biggest difference is the amount of exposure you get to language, experiences, extra curricular activities, etc. Private schools believe heavily in a complete education process, continuous learning through a variety of platforms. It can be as simple as library visits or more sophisticated enrichment activities like: dance/music lessons, art classes, cooking classes, camps specialized in math, science, computers, etc. or even class trips abroad to learn about other cultures. All of these experiences build up by the end of high school and can make a difference when applying to college. Parents who cannot send their children to private school can try to implement some of these same types of principles by adding on to the standard education experiences (standard school day). Parents should realize that when they don't know something, somebody else does. The key is to find that person to help their kids and get started as early as possible because preparation is vital for higher levels of academia."

Requirements

In order for students to graduate from high school, they need to have a certain number of points or credits on their record. The way to get these credits is by taking classes. In most high schools, one semester of a course equals ½ a credit. Students' schedules are organized so that they can complete all the courses they need to graduate in four years. Some of those courses are required by the State Board of Education and some are chosen according to students' own interests. Unlike the way things work in Latin America where students usually have to take a fixed number of courses per year, in the U.S. there are many courses that can be taken at different times during the four years. The goal is to pass all the required courses and all tests required by the state in order to graduate. For example, New York has the Regents exams that students take during the four years of high school. Usually, they take science in ninth grade, math in tenth, global studies in eleventh, and social studies and English in twelfth. It would be good for you to find out what tests are required in your state to get a high school diploma.

Attendance

Depending on the courses they take, students' schedules will vary, which means it's harder to monitor their school attendance than it was in elementary school when they always began classes at the same time. It is very important that you make sure your child attends school every day because:

■ Most high schools have policies that require students to limit their absences to receive full credit for a class or to avoid having their grade reduced, sometimes by an entire letter grade. (They would get a B instead of an A, for example.)

- Many employers look at attendance records when making hiring decisions. It helps them predict your child's likely performance at work.

- Many schools penalize students with poor attendance records by not allowing them to attend career classes, which may be of great interest to your child in the future.

- The only way to learn and prepare for college is to attend school. By cutting classes, your children are putting their futures at risk.

- If they are cutting class, they may be getting into trouble.

Your job as the parent is to make sure that they attend class every day. This also means that you should avoid taking your kids out of school for vacations, to work, or for any other reason. **Remember**: finishing high school is only the first step to move ahead in this country. You need to support this process.

Expert to Parent

"Parents should look at school attendance and period attendance. They need to ask: 'Did my child attend every period (class)? Is my child allowed to leave the building between periods?' Don't wait for the report card to find out if they are attending classes, ask for an interim report. Find out who in the school is in charge of your child's attendance and stay in touch with that person," recommends Michael Kohlhagen, Superintendent of Wethersfield Public Schools.

Grades and Grade Point Average

Understanding the grade system is more crucial than you can imagine as it is both what will be used to measure your children when they are applying for college and when they are competing for scholarships and other special programs. The grade point average (GPA) is the average of all of your child's class grades. Each grade they get for a class has a point value.

Here are the equivalents:

A = 4.0 points, or 90-100

B = 3.0 points, or 80-89

C = 2.0 points or 75-79

D = 1.0 points or 70-74

F = .9 or below, or below 70

There are some variations to this table; some schools assign point values for minuses and pluses (*i.e.* A- = 3.8). Others assign more points to a B in an honors course (because it's more demanding) than in a regular course.

When students take a course and fail it, they don't get credit, and it doesn't count towards graduation. Even though some schools may remove a low grade from students' averages if they retake the class, many don't; so that failure will affect their GPA permanently.

Keep in mind that the better the college, the higher the GPA it requires.

In terms of scholarships, most of them have a minimum GPA requirement. Again, the higher your child's GPA, the more options he or she will have when the time comes to apply for grants and special programs.

College Graduate to Parent

María D. Soldevilla, who graduated in 2005 with her Master in Business Administration and currently works in pharmaceutical sales, says: "I found out in my senior year in high school that there was a system called GPA based on a 4.0 scale. Had I known about this scale I would have known what I was being measured on and I would have made a conscious effort to keep my score perfect." María worked hard her senior year to raise her GPA from a 3.7 to a 3.8 so she could apply to the Presidential Scholarship at Friends University in Wichita, Kansas, which she received. She then went on to graduate college where she maintained a perfect 4.0, setting the bar quite high for her four younger siblings.

Learn About Key Exams and Programs

There are many important exams and programs that will improve a student's potential for successfully making it to college. Becoming acquainted with them will help you encourage your children when it is their time to take on the challenge.

PSAT Test

PSAT stands for *Preliminary Scholastic Assessment Test*. It is a standardized test that provides firsthand practice for the *Scholastic Assessment Test* (SAT), one of the factors that colleges evaluate when reviewing applications. Educators highly recommend that your tenth-grader take the PSAT exams because they serve as a good diagnostic tool to identify strengths and weaknesses early on.

The PSAT measures:

- critical reading skills;

- math problem-solving skills; and,

- writing skills.

Bear in mind that students develop these skills over many years, both in and out of school. As a matter of fact, research shows that the best way to prepare for these tests is by reading thirty minutes a day from elementary school on, as vocabulary and reading comprehension develop over time. There are many reasons for encouraging your children to take this test, but the following are the most important ones:

- To receive feedback on your children's strengths and weaknesses on skills necessary for college study.

- To see how your children's performance on an admissions test might compare with that of others applying to college.

- To enter the competition for scholarships from the *National Merit Scholarship* Corporation, which are awarded in eleventh grade.

- To help prepare for the SAT, the results of which are used as part of the college application process. Your children can become familiar with the kinds of questions and the exact directions they will see on the SAT.

PLAN

PLAN is the *Pre-American College Test* (ACT). Just like the PSAT, it identifies your children's academic strengths and weaknesses so they can work with their teachers and counselors on a plan to improve weak areas. As not every school offers this test, and it is a preview of the ACT, if your children's school doesn't offer it, they should ask their counselor to take it at a school that does. If there is none available nearby, for a small fee, ACT will send them the test so they can take it in their own school.

Inspirational Capsule

Warlene Gary, CEO of the National PTA, shares these words: "The research speaks for itself—kids whose parents are involved in their education do better all around. And the research on resiliency shows that kids who do well against all odds have a caring adult in their lives. Parents have the responsibility to make sure they are involved in their children's lives."

Regular Honors Programs, Advanced Placement (AP), and International Baccalaureate (IB)

Local high school teachers develop regular honors courses to help meet the needs of accelerated students. Although these courses tend to offer the same curriculum as non-honors classes, they are more challenging and cover topics more in-depth. However, students cannot generally earn college credit through these classes because they are not considered to be college level classes.

Advanced Placement (AP) courses, however, may allow a high school student to earn college credit. Along with the results of the PSAT, the teacher gets what is called an *AP potential* for each student, telling him or her which students are the most likely to do well in college. If your children are amongst them, they can enroll in an AP program where they will be able to take courses that will prepare them for the type of work done in college. These courses are more difficult and involve harder work than standard classes. They are developed by teachers and college faculty with the help of the College Board. Because they are considered college-level courses, students may be able to earn credits towards college if they obtain a certain score on the AP exam at the end of the course, depending on what university they decide to attend.

Not all schools offer AP classes, so talk to your child's principal. In the event that AP classes are not offered in your children's school, find out if they can participate online. Visit the College Board's website (**www.collegeboard.com**) for more information.

Many schools offer the *International Baccalaureate* (IB) program developed by the *International Baccalaureate Organization* (**www.ibo.org**). This organization works with international organizations, governments, and schools to create a challenging program to give students a wider perspective of the world they live in. If your child is highly motivated, he or she can take the prestigious IB Diploma Program for the final two years of high school. It is a very hard program that ends with exams in six different subject areas. In order to obtain college credit, students must obtain a specific score on these tests. To find out if your child's school offers the program, visit IB's website.

Benefits
As a parent, it is important for you to help your children decide whether they should take Advance Placement courses. It will require hard work, but it has many benefits for your children:

■   get a head start on college-level work;

■   improve their writing skills and sharpen their problem-solving techniques;

■   develop the study habits necessary for tackling rigorous course work;

■   stand out in the college admissions process;

■   demonstrate maturity and readiness for college;

■   show willingness to push themselves to the limit;

■   explore the world from a variety of perspectives, including their own;

■   study subjects in greater depth and detail;

■   assume the responsibility of reasoning, analyzing, and understanding for themselves; and,

■   improve their GPA. Because these classes are harder than non-honors classes, the grades obtained in honors courses are usually given an extra point. So, in the standard four-point grading system where A = 4 grade points, B = 3 grade points, C = 2 grade points, etc., in honors courses your child will usually be earning A = 5 points, B = 4 points and C = 3 points.

Currently, several colleges are re-evaluating whether to exempt students with AP credit from certain classes and others are asking students to take introductory courses even if they passed an AP exam on the same subject.

Generally speaking, however, AP courses as well as the IB program are more rigorous than regular courses and they will raise the bar for your children's achievement.

Therefore, it is a good idea for you and your kids to seriously consider them.

Inspirational Capsule

"The way I keep my mind motivated is by visualizing what I could have with a high school and a college education—a very nice car, a good house, many trips, you know what money could give you," says Eduardo A. García, 11th-grader from Austin High School in El Paso, Texas.

Special Programs on Your Child's Campus: Junior Achievement Worldwide

Many high schools offer special programs during the year that your children can get involved in. These programs are usually offered by outside organizations in partnership with the school. A great example is *Junior Achievement Worldwide* (**www.ja.org**) that provides basic understanding of business, free enterprise, and economics to students from kindergarten through 12th grade. The high school segment is seven to eight weeks long, one hour per week, and it runs in schools thanks to the volunteer facilitators—business owners, retired business people, parents just like yourself—who teach the classes. Usually the program is implemented in a social studies, economics, or business class, but it can also take place after school. Some teachers may give extra credit for participation.

Gloria Esteban, the director of High School Programs of Junior Achievement of Central Florida, mentions that students who go through the program improve their business skills, something very valuable to Latinos who are natural entrepreneurs. "Students role play applying for a job, they develop interview skills, interpersonal effectiveness, problem solving skills, and many other important skills that will help them in the future."

There is also a special 24-week program called *JA Company Program* where, under the supervision of volunteer business consultants, students learn to run, manage, and liquidate their own small business. They get to choose if they want to develop a company based on a product or a service and the lessons they learn range from developing a board of directors to selling stock to choosing high level personnel for their company.

In 2006, JA Worldwide launched its Hispanic Initiative pilot program. Its goal is to engage Hispanic communities by increasing the number of Hispanic volunteers and students who participate in JA Worldwide programs. This initiative—which is currently being implemented in Los Angeles, New York, Denver, Atlanta, and Albuquerque—will provide more students across the U.S. with hands-on learning experiences designed to inspire and prepare them for success in the global economy.

If your child's school doesn't offer Junior Achievement programs there are a few things you may want to do: you can ask the school to connect with JA's Area Office to discuss the possibility of setting up some programs, you can volunteer to be trained and then teach one of the programs yourself, or you can encourage your employer to sponsor a JA program in your child's school.

SATs and ACTs

Regarding the SAT, the only difference from the PSAT is the format. The type of questions and techniques that apply to the PSAT also apply to the SAT.

Several experts say that many Latino parents are not aware of the importance of sending their children to SAT and ACT preparation courses where they learn how to take the test. You have to realize that these tests require certain skills that children may not have, even if they are great students.

The SAT is administered seven times a year—usually in October, November, December, January, March, May, and June—on Saturday mornings. The ACT, a test similar to the SAT, is administered six times a year—usually September, October, December, February, April, and June—also on Saturday mornings. To find out more details about the SAT, visit the College Board website at **www.collegeboard.com**. For more information on the ACT, visit ACT, Inc.'s website at **www.act.org**. Both sites have a Spanish section where you can read details about the test.

Students can ask their teachers for practice tests or they can find many for free on websites like **www.thebeehive.org**, **www.collegeboard.com**, and **www.act.org**. There are also many practice books available at the bookstore. Take into consideration that using practice tests should be complemented by attending test preparation classes.

It is crucial that your children take either the SAT or the ACT because, even though colleges consider other factors as well, the competition for admission is so great that every single element counts.

Despite the fact that students can take either one of these tests as often as they want, even though some schools will average their scores, most students are better off preparing thoroughly for the test, taking it once, and getting their top score. You or your children should call the universities to which they will be applying to find out their policy on multiple scores.

Inspirational Capsule

Abe Tomás Hughes II, CEO of Hispanic Alliance for Career Enhancement (HACE), was born to Mexican parents in a border town. He is the only one of four siblings who went to college, and he graduated with an MBA from Harvard. "In Latin America there is a caste system. If you were born poor, it's very difficult to get out of poverty because there is very little social mobility. That's the difference with the U.S. where, if you study, you can change your socioeconomic status. I see it in my own family; I look back on my life and I see how different it is from that of my siblings."

Tracking, Streaming, Ability Grouping

Tracking, streaming, or ability grouping means that students are grouped according to their ability in a particular subject. For example, there may be two different math classes, a low track and a high track. Although some tracking takes place in many elementary and middle schools as well, high school is usually when students are tracked most.

In recent years, there has been a lot of controversy over the tracking of students' abilities, because some research shows that minorities are disproportionately represented in the lower track. Because these lower tracks have been shown to lead to lower achievement in later years, it is important that you become informed about this issue. Another important aspect to take into account is that being consistently placed in the lower tracks may lower your child's self esteem and conse-quently lower his or her academic performance.

Some experts believe that grouping students according to their abilities helps the high-track students because they get better teachers who can challenge them with more difficult material, whereas it is less beneficial to low-track students who are not pushed hard enough. Other experts think that, on the contrary, when students of homogeneous abilities are in the same class, which is what tracking does, they learn more because the material is targeted to their level.

One thing is true, though. The children of parents who are on top of this issue—who get help in math and science for their children, and who talk to the teacher about how their children can improve in these areas—tend to be placed in higher tracks. Because educated parents are very aware of how much the high tracks have helped them in their own educational careers, they are the most vocal about having their children placed in the high track. That is why, in order to give your children more opportunities, you need to become well-versed on this topic. If your children's school tracks students, ask your PTA for literature on the subject.

Expert to Parent

Patricia Garrity, principal of Cristo Rey High School in Chicago, IL, which offers an extremely successful work program, suggests that the secret to the success of her school is the sense of community it created. "We have an *asesoría* (advisory) structure. Groups of about 17 students meet with an *asesor* (advisor) for half an hour every day. The asesor is a guidance counselor, an academic counselor, and a career counselor. This is also the person who looks at their report cards and helps them set goals. It's also the first person parents go to when they have a question. The groups go out with their asesor to have pizza together, they organize outings... It's all part of our commitment to be a smaller school," Garrity shares.

Volunteering

In most Latin American countries there is no culture of volunteering for organizations, something that is very common in the U.S. and very beneficial for high school kids.

Spending time at the local hospital, at a Latin American organization, at a program for special education kids, or in any other place helps children develop many valuable skills. They learn responsibility, troubleshooting, leadership skills, time management, social skills, and many job related abilities. Volunteering is not only important because colleges look into it as part of their application requirements, but because it's a great way to keep youngsters focused on a positive activity and away from trouble. Achieving success in the activity of their choice contributes to strong self-esteem which is the basis for strong academic performance. Help them figure out where they could channel their passions while they lend a hand where it's needed. For example, if your kids like music, maybe they can volunteer at a radio station's fundraising event; if they are good with computers, perhaps they can teach basic email skills to Latino immigrants at the local library. Look for opportunities in Chapter 4: Extracurricular Activities and Summer Programs.

Chapter 3

Other Ways to Fulfill High School Requirements

If for some reason your children can't fulfill their requirements during regular school hours, they may want to explore some alternative options for completing high school.

Long Distance Learning

Although this may be the best alternative for your children, be aware that for all the benefits that studying on their own time frame affords them, they will lose a valuable element of attending high school—the social interaction with other children, an important component of a teenager's development.

That being said, some states allow students to take long distance credit courses over the Internet to fulfill their high school requirements. These are high schools that offer a similar array of courses as the ones offered in regular high schools. They provide an alternative that helps your children overcome any time or geographic constraints that may prevent them from completing high school. Each course is usually designed around a study guide, textbook, and exams and the instructors provide students responses to their assignments and tests through email. Students who choose this alternative need to be self-motivated because, although studying at home on their own schedule can make things easier for them, it also demands a greater sense of responsibility. You can visit the site of one of the accreditation organizations to find a list of schools that offer programs online: **www.detc.org**. One of these schools is Keystone National High School (**www.keystonehighschool.com**), a private high school. Your children can take individual courses or sign up to be full time students. You will find the prices on the school's website as well.

You can also find a list of high schools with online programs at **www.online-education.net**.

Expert to Parent

Dr. Donald Carlisle, Superintendent of Port Chester Public Schools in Port Chester, NY, suggests that one way to accelerate a student who comes from a different country and has entered high school late is through an online program. "If a student is two grades behind, the key is to accelerate. Summer school, independent study and taking courses for credit on the Internet are all good ways to accomplish that. In many cases, the public school that the child attends may have the funds to pay for those online courses if they help students catch up and graduate on time."

As you read on, you will realize that every decision you and your children make during high school should be made with an eye on college. Online courses can be the perfect solution for the right situation. For example, if yours is a migrant family and your children transfer schools several times a year, their best alternative to finish high school may be to do so through an online program. Any admissions officer would understand this story. Think about it—this child, instead of hiding behind his or her circumstances and not finishing school, overcame that difficulty with great sacrifice and found a way to graduate. This is the kind of redemption story that admissions officers love to hear. Read more about this issue in Chapter 9: What Do Colleges Look for in an Applicant.

Night School

Some states call it night school, others call it alternative school, but whatever the name, this is a good option for students who are working, or can't complete their requirements during the regular school day. It also offers a great way to accelerate your child's graduation if he or she has the time to attend night school and day school at the same time. Again, ask your children to find out if this is an alternative available at their school.

GED

If your child hasn't graduated from high school, he or she may take a test that certifies that he or she has an understanding of reading, writing, social studies, science, and math. Minimum age requirements for taking the GED differ in each state, but range from age 16 to 18. Once your child passes this test, he or she will get the *General Educational Development* certificate or GED. There are courses and books that can prepare your children to take this test that is offered in numerous places very frequently during the year. The

GED Test can be taken in English, Spanish, French, and Vietnamese.

The test is usually taken over a period of two or three days and it tests five areas: writing, reading, math, science, and social studies.

If your family moves a lot, your children may find it difficult to finish high school. Taking the GED is a good step for them to continue their education and go on to college. Keep in mind, however, that even if your children have transferred schools often, they can still earn their high school diploma.

If your child is having trouble completing his or her graduation requirements and is approaching 21, you should encourage him or her to have a serious discussion with the school's guidance counselor about taking the GED.

Most employers consider the GED diploma to be an equivalent of a high school diploma. A few of them regard it less favorably. Once the student has a college degree, however, people tend to overlook how they completed high school.

Some Worrisome Statistics

You need to know that the high school completion rate for Latinos is much lower than that of all other populations. According to 2004 data from the National Center for Education Statistics of the United States Education Department, the percentage of 16- to 24-year-olds who are not enrolled in high school and don't have a high school diploma is 6.8% for whites; 11.8% for African Americans; and 23% for Hispanics. This number is higher for Hispanics born outside of the U.S.—38.4%— and lower for first and second generation of Hispanics born in the U.S—14.7% and 13.7% respectively.

According to the White House Initiative on Education Excellence for Hispanic Americans, one in every three Hispanic students does not complete high school, and only 10% of Hispanics graduate from four-year colleges and universities. According to the Pew Hispanic Center, by the time they are 26 years old, only 43% of Hispanic dropouts have received a GED compared to 50% of white dropouts. Although there are several theories regarding this educational gap, there are a number of reasons that can contribute to these appalling statistics:

- Students see limited job possibilities after high school because jobs are not available where they live. They may think education does not pay off.

- Minority students may feel alienated from the school context. They do not feel validated, because their cultural background is not understood or embraced by the school. Their second language is not seen as strength.

- Students may see opportunities to get into the workforce now, and they may not see that the long-term consequence of not having a high school diploma is a lack of upward mobility.

- Children do not feel successful in school. They do not have ties with adults—teachers or guidance counselors—who could make them feel successful. They would rather get out and find something to do where they can feel good about themselves.

- They do not feel a sense of community at school. They feel a sense of community at home or with a gang.

- Parents believe that education is important, but that making money is more important.

Expert to Parent

"Parents should start talking to their kids about college in kindergarten. They should talk about goals, careers, different educational levels of various occupations; they should set high standards. Once kids get older, parents should encourage them to use career inventory programs available as software. They help students see what careers match their interest. All high schools have this software, it's just a question of kids asking for it," suggests Michael Kohlhagen, Superintendent of Wethersfield Public Schools.

Chapter 4

Extracurricular Activities and Summer Programs

Extracurricular Activities

Extracurricular activities are a great way for your child to gain an advantage in the college admissions process. Admission departments not only look for academic accomplishment, but for students who participate in other activities such as clubs or sports teams. Colleges want to know what students do once they close their textbooks for the day. Does the student play video games all day or volunteer at a community center in the afternoon? The point of joining extracurricular activities, however, is not to fill a resume with countless clubs to prove the student did *something* during the four years in high school. The activities chosen should reflect your child's commitments and passions, and the final resume should represent his or her accomplishments both in academics and extracurricular activities.

The best time to join a club, a team, or a program is at the beginning of the school year. Encourage your child to check the school bulletin board or the school newspaper to find the different activities offered at the high school. They usually offer a variety of clubs such as photography, chess, bowling, or art, and academic clubs for students interested in science or math. There are also clubs that reflect different cultures. Many local organizations have high school clubs for those who would like to volunteer and get involved. If your child is interested in a particular activity that is not offered at the school, you may help him or her check the local newspaper for any information, ask other parents, or have your child ask other students where to find this type of activity.

If your child has a specific goal, such as becoming a math teacher, find an activity that will support those interests. For example, he or she can volunteer at the local community center and tutor younger children in math. If he or she is interested in sports management, he or she can become involved in the youth sports leagues and assist coaches. However, if your child does not have a specific goal in mind yet, you should encourage him or her to volunteer at local organizations like the community center, the hospital, the library, and other local non-profit organizations which are always looking for a helping hand.

Extracurricular activities are beneficial to students for many reasons. Students learn the values of teamwork, responsibility, and they develop leadership skills. It also helps students in managing their time by learning to juggle these out-of-school activities and academics.

Time management is a necessary tool to develop while in high school, in order to succeed in college and in life by keeping high academic standards, yet having time to relax.

But because the pressure to succeed academically and to fulfill extracurricular responsibilities can be overwhelming, you don't want your children to be spread too thin. This could have a negative effect both on academics and their health. So, make sure you help your child make wise choices when it comes to selecting appropriate activities.

Here are some organizations that welcome volunteers. Pass on the websites to your children so they can get more information before they decide to get involved.

A Few Interesting Programs

YMCA (www.ymca.net)

With over two thousand locations worldwide, the YMCA is a volunteer organization that works to build strong families and strong communities. There are five categories of volunteers: program, support, fundraising, policy, and managerial.

Boys and Girls Clubs of America (www.bgca.org)

The Boys and Girls Club of America works to provide a positive environment for children and offers support and a sense of belonging. Your child can help with hands-on activities and be a role model.

Habitat for Humanity (www.habitat.org)

Habitat offers a variety of volunteer programs. Help construct homes, assist with fundraising, and give back to the community. Your child should find out if his or her high school already has a *Habitat Chapter*—a student-led organization which partnered with Habitat for Humanity—and ask how to get involved. Ideal if your children like architecture, engineering, etc.

Smithsonian Institution (www.si.edu/volunteer)
The Smithsonian Institute offers many programs for volunteer service. Volunteers are given the opportunity to enhance the museum experience for visitors by assisting with hands-on activities, providing staff with support, and much more.

Latino Commission on AIDS (www.latinoaids.org)
Dedicate a few hours a month and make a difference. Help raise funds, raise awareness, and gather support for important changes in AIDS policy.

National Audubon Society (www.audubon.org)
The Audubon Society has several chapters and nature-centers all over the United States that are working to conserve and restore natural ecosystems. Locate the nearest Audubon center and find out how you can help. Ideal if your children are interested in nature, animals, or the environment.

Junior Achievement Worldwide (www.ja.org)
This organization provides basic understanding of business, free enterprise, and economics to students from kindergarten through 12th grade. Your children can become part of their *High School Heroes program* through which they teach JA classes to younger students. Great to help your kids develop leadership skills and improve their self esteem. It's also wonderful for students interested in business and in opening their own companies.

Summer Programs

When summer arrives, most students just want to relax and hang out with their friends. They want to leave the pressures of the school year behind and enjoy the break.

But summer is a great opportunity to get involved with the community, travel, and develop valuable skills. As you will see in the next few chapters, all extra curricular activities and summer programs can build your children's high school resume to make their college admissions process easier. Students who have a passion and who have been consistently involved with certain activities or programs, make for much stronger candidates when filling out a college application.

There are several colleges and universities that offer summer programs specifically designed for high school students. They give students the chance to experience college life by participating in campus activities, living in residence halls, and enrolling in college courses. Your teenagers will meet other high school students with similar interests and build friendships. Many of these colleges offer college credit on completion of the program, but some do not.

Many organizations offer programs that revolve around community service and leadership, as well as academics. There are also summer programs that cater to the arts, computer science, culture, dance, and sports. Don't limit your children's options to programs in the U.S. There are many summer programs abroad that can greatly expand your child's view of the world and be extremely valuable for their education. No matter what your children's interests are there is a summer program or camp out there that will fit their needs.

A Few Interesting Programs

I'm including here some interesting resources, but you should not limit yourself or your children to these. There are hundreds of programs you can tap into. Just ask your child's guidance counselor to help you do additional research or talk to the librarian at the local library. There are scholarships and financial aid available for many of the camps and programs listed here, so get in touch with each one and find out their policy. Do not think that you can't afford a program from the way it sounds. Call them and find out the cost and whether they have financial aid available to you.

Here are some websites and books where you can find more information on summer programs.

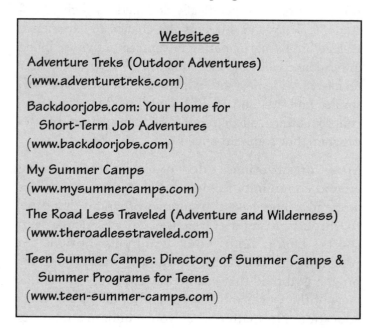

Websites

Adventure Treks (Outdoor Adventures)
(www.adventuretreks.com)

Backdoorjobs.com: Your Home for
  Short-Term Job Adventures
(www.backdoorjobs.com)

My Summer Camps
(www.mysummercamps.com)

The Road Less Traveled (Adventure and Wilderness)
(www.theroadlesstraveled.com)

Teen Summer Camps: Directory of Summer Camps &
  Summer Programs for Teens
(www.teen-summer-camps.com)

Examples of Summer Programs

Academic Study Associates at University of Massachusetts-Amherst
(www.asaprograms.com)

This summer program provides high school students with challenging academic courses and a range of activities that will enhance their summer experience. There is a wide selection of college credit and enrichment courses ranging from business and economics to Latin dance. A number of weekend trips are organized to show students the best of New England.

America's Adventure Ventures Everywhere (AAVE): Teen Adventures
(www.aave.com)

AAVE provides summer programs that will cater to any student's interest—academic, adventure, community service, study aboard, and travel. Students can choose from a variety of programs offered in several countries. There are programs in the United States, Latin America, Europe, Asia, Africa, and Australia. Your kids can choose to snowboard or ski in Switzerland, go backpacking in the French Alps, mountain bike on the Andean volcanoes in Ecuador, or become immersed in a foreign language. Programs require mental and physical toughness, patience, and commitment.

College Bridge Program—Northwestern University
(www.scs.northwestern.edu/summernu)

This program is open to high school juniors in the Chicago Public School System. Students will enroll in one undergraduate course and receive college credit. Taking classes with Northwestern undergraduates, will give your teenagers valuable experience on academic and social life on campus.

Early Start Program—
University of California Santa Barbara
(www.summer.ucsb.edu)
Students in the 10th, 11th, or 12th grades are welcome to participate in this fun and exciting academic program. Students will enroll in two undergraduate courses that cater to their interests. The program's objective is to increase the student's competitiveness when applying to other universities in the nation.

High School Summer Institute—
Columbia College Chicago
(www.colum.edu)
This five week program is designed for high school sophomores, juniors, and seniors who want to learn more about the visual, media, and communication arts. Your kids will be encouraged to explore their ideas and creative thinking by using a number of on-campus facilities—art studios, graphic design labs, film and video production studios, and much more. The campus is in the heart of downtown Chicago.

Honor College Pre-Collegiate Institute—
Florida International University
(http://honors.fiu.edu/program_collegiate.htm)
This challenging summer program offers students the opportunity to enroll in college courses the summer prior to their senior year in high school. Students must be Florida residents to be eligible for this program.

Latino Community Leadership Seminar—
University of Notre Dame
(www.nd.edu/~precoll)
Explore the role of Latinos in U.S. society through a series of presentations and discussions. Your teenagers will gain a deeper understanding of Latino

culture values, learn important leadership skills, and develop a strong commitment to community service. They will also have access to recreational sports facilities, off-campus activities and social events.

Leadership Experience
(www.learningtolead.org)

This one-week summer experience is ideal for students who want to develop their leadership skills. The program is open to students in grades 8 through 12. During the week, kids will participate in exciting projects, interactive workshops, and skill-building sessions. These activities will focus on critical leadership topics, such us negotiation, decision-making, and motivation. By the end of the week, your kids will have developed key skills for success.

Putney Student Travel
(www.goputney.com)

Putney Student Travel is open to high school students, in grades 9 through 12, who are looking for a fun, challenging, and educational summer. These programs put an emphasis on community service, global awareness, and cultural exploration. Putney offers programs in several countries all over the world, including Ecuador, Madagascar, and India. Your children are given the opportunity to learn about a new culture by getting involved in the community.

Senior Enrichment Program—Julian Krinsky
Camps and Program
(www.jkcp.com)

This program is a great opportunity to experience college life. Your children can attend classes in the arts, business, SAT Prep, and many other subjects along with sports activities, trips and special programs.

Student Leaders in Service—
Birmingham Southern College
(www.bsc.edu)

This week-long residential program exposes high school students to leadership theories, and opportunities to practice leadership through several community service activities. Your kids will also get a taste of college life by living in the residence halls, participating in on-campus activities, and meeting current students. The program welcomes students the summer prior to their senior year in high school.

Summer College for High School Students—
Syracuse University
(www.summercollege.syr.edu)

This six week program for high school juniors and seniors gives students a taste of academic and social college life. Credit hours are given on the successful completion of the courses.

SuperCamp—Senior Forum
(www.qln.com/supercamp.aspx)

At this academic summer program, your children will learn their strengths, pursue goals, develop skills to increase test scores, and ease school stress. There is also a Parents' Weekend that is designed to teach parents the skills their children learn so that they are better able to relate to their son or daughter after the SuperCamp experience.

Books

Peterson's Summer Opportunities for Kids & Teenagers
A terrific book listing over a thousand summer camps and programs, ranging from art clinics to wilderness adventures.

The Princeton Review: The 500 Best Ways for Teens to Spend the Summer
A great guide for exciting and educational summer programs.

Chapter 5

Parent Involvement in High School

High school is a very difficult time for kids, and even more so if they were not raised in this country. At this age, adolescents are more independent, they are searching for their identity, their need to belong to a group is exacerbated, and they are willing to try different things. They are also more susceptible to bad influences. All good reasons for you to remain involved in their education and in their lives even when teenagers are reluctant to allow their parents to have an opinion about anything.

One of the areas you should be involved in is the balance between your children's social life and their school work. As important as it is to encourage kids to spend time with other youngsters, high school is also a time to focus on hard work. Grades are increasingly important for your kids to have more opportunities to go to the colleges they choose and to get scholarships.

Expert to Parent

Charles Strange, principal of Cherry Valley-Springfield Junior Senior High School in Cherry Valley, New York, emphasizes that schools can not be successful if parents are not partners in guiding students. "I would like to see parents more involved in raising their children's aspirations. We also want them to expose kids to career opportunities that they as parents have experienced," he says.

Identifying Mentors

Another area in which you should get involved is in finding *mentors* for your children. (Mentors are people who guide and help others along the way.) If you can't guide your kids through high school as much as you would like to, help them find people who can. It can be someone in your family or the family of one of your children's friends. Look for a person who understands the education system well and ask him or her to help you with your children's questions. You may also want to identify several people who have interesting careers and occupations about which your children may want to learn more. There's nothing better for students to get a clear picture of what a job entails than spending some time with a person who is doing that job. If you can't identify a mentor for your child, don't worry. In most communities there are several mentoring programs that you can tap into, like *Big Brothers and Big Sisters* (**www.bbbs.org**) for example. You can also find many mentoring programs on this website: **www.islandnet.com/~rcarr/mentorprograms.html**.

You should also talk to your child's guidance counselor or school principal and ask for suggestions. If you don't get a satisfactory answer, visit your local library and talk to the librarian.

Remember that developing a close relationship with adults who serve as mentors is a great way for children to stay the course, and many times, it's easier for kids to listen to adults who are not their parents. Just make sure you know the adults well before you trust them with your kids.

Parent to Parent

Alfonso Zhicay, father of a 15-year-old daughter who has received many awards, says, "The biggest challenge I face with my child right now is dealing with the stuff her peers offer her, like drugs. I have found ways to talk to her, to show her the pros and cons." Zhicay's suggestion to counteract the influence of peers is to stay involved: "My wife and I attend every school meeting and in addition, I go by the school twice a month to talk to the counselor. I find out how she is doing and about her attendance."

Keeping Communication Channels Open

Being involved with your children's education means that you should consider being a PTA member just as when your children were younger. It also means that you have to maintain as open a dialog with your kids as possible. The more you talk to them, the more you listen to them, the more in-tune you are with their activities, their obligations, and their concerns, the less likely it will be that your children will get into trouble. "There are some family values that are escaping many

American families at this time, but that still exist in other countries," explains Mr. Strange from Cherry Valley-Springfield Junior Senior High School. "Families need to eat dinner together. They need a time, a place, and a reason to sit down and talk and this should be the rule and not the exception. I blame the TV and the microwave for this change, and I also blame our obsession with keeping kids busy since it is often this continual *activity treadmill* that denies parents the quality time they need to be spending directly with their children."

In the last few years there has been a lot of research connecting the increase risk factors in children who live in homes where the family doesn't have a meal together every day. The Latino culture values food and family so much, that if this is a tradition that got lost in your home, you should try to reinstate it as soon as possible. Make sure the entire family sits for dinner every night— keep the TV off to encourage conversation and take the opportunity to share what the day was like for each one of you. Get in the habit of telling each other stories.

Marcela Hoffer, a clinical social worker, suggests that keeping an open dialog is not only about talking: "If parents realize that their kid loves baseball for example, they should sit down with them to watch a game. If they share an interest, even without talking, the child will feel understood and not alone."

Expert to Parent

Ana C. Ansin, Instructional Officer of the Migrant Education Program at El Paso Independent School District, comments, "The larger obstacle that Latino kids in this area face in high school is poverty. The majority of the students that I work with come from very low socioeconomic households where parents have not had an opportunity of completing elementary school and some of them are illiterate. Their children don't have a strong foundation in their first language which makes it even more difficult to learn a second language. Because language is an obstacle for many of them, their self esteem and confidence is affected and so are their social skills. Because their parents have but the minimum education and lack exposure to a different way of life, some of them don't even know that education is the only tool that their kids need to break the cycle of poverty and succeed."

As you see, Ana's comments go hand in hand with Martín Curiel's story with which I started off this book.

Choosing Courses

In order for students to get all the necessary credits for graduation, they need to have a plan. Your mission should be to get involved in the plan early on in order to help them meet the graduation requirements.

By looking together at the list of course offerings, you can discuss with your children the different possibilities. For example, if the school requires two credits of history or social studies, they may be able to choose between American History, World History, Ancient

History, etc. You may suggest certain subjects based on your children's interests and where they could be headed in the future. Again, if you feel that you are not the best person to help them make these kinds of decisions, try to find them someone who can guide them.

When evaluating courses, encourage your children to choose more difficult classes. Not only will they help them to develop strong academic skills, which are crucial for students aiming to go to college, but they will keep them more engaged. Sometimes kids may choose easier classes just because their friends are taking them or so they don't have to work so hard. But you know, from your own experience, that when you coast at work, you pay for it later. Help them evaluate the advantages of taking honors courses, Advanced Placement classes, and the International Baccalaureate program.

Also, make sure you speak up if your child gets placed into a class he or she didn't request or is below his or her abilities. Many times, parents are more persuasive than students when it comes to issues like this, so make your voice heard if your child is not getting the attention he or she deserves. The best idea is to intervene quickly because these changes should be done very early in the semester.

Getting to Know the Teachers

It's essential for you to become familiar with the school personnel from day one. You need to know not just your child's teachers but every adult in the building who is involved with your child in any way. Different schools have different structures. Some may have deans, department chairs, attendance officers, peer counselors, guidance counselors, a center for new arrivals, etc. Understanding the structure will help you access it with ease whenever you need to. If you develop a strong relationship with all these people and have the habit of dropping by at your child's school at any time, both your son or daughter and the teachers will get the message that you have high expectations for your child and that you are there if they need you.

Special Education in High School

It is interesting how Anglo parents will fight to get their children evaluated if there is even the slightest suspicion that they may need special education, and how they fight to get the school to provide the extra help immediately and throughout their high school career. In contrast, Latino parents tend to react negatively when they are told that their children may need to receive special services. In many instances they refuse to have their children evaluated, and they also refuse the additional help that the school is offering.

Expert to Parent

Dr. Donald Carlisle, the Superintendent, suggests that if parents have any concerns about their children needing extra help, they should have their kids tested. "Some parents who don't trust the school should have their children tested by an outside professional. So, if they feel more comfortable, they should have their children tested by a Latino professional and bring the results to school. The other idea is that they find a Latino advocate in the school and talk to that person."

Children don't develop learning disabilities or any other disability overnight. So, if your child is entering the American school system for the first time at the high school level, and he or she has a disability he or she should have already been identified as in need of special services. However, according to Anthony Bellettieri, school psychologist at the middle and high school levels, many students who enter school speaking no English may slip through the system without being identified in need of special education until high school just because they don't speak the language yet and people think that is the problem.

Whatever the specifics of your situation, if you notice your children having any difficulties—in communicating, understanding, hearing, or in behavioral, emotional, psychological, or motor skills—you should inform the teachers right away. The idea is for your child to be evaluated immediately so that the problem can be identified and your child can begin receiving services. By law, if your child's first language is Spanish, he or she should be evaluated in Spanish by a native speaker. And also by law, the school can not evaluate your child without your consent.

Expert to Parent

Jessica O'Donovan, director of a large ESL program, explains: "If your child requires special education services and the school doesn't have a bilingual special education teacher, you should ask the school or the district how they plan to address both his learning needs as well as his language needs. For example, the school might choose to hire a bilingual teacher's aide to

> work along the teacher and provide native language support as needed. Every situation is different, but the important point is to make sure the instructional program fully meets the needs of your child."

In this country there is a huge array of services available to students with any kind of disability. The idea is for them to receive these services in the least restrictive environment, which means that whenever possible it is better for the student to attend a regular class where a second teacher works with him or her one-on-one. Another alternative may be that the child is taken out of the classroom for a period to work on a specific subject where he or she needs reinforcement. Children who are severely disabled may be placed in a separate class.

What is important for you to take into consideration is that you are the most important advocate for your children. If they need extra help, you need to work on getting it for them. So, first approach the teachers. If you don't get a satisfactory solution to the problem, talk to the principal, and if this still doesn't work, talk to the person at the district office who is in charge of special education. Don't stop until you get your child the help he or she needs!

A Word on Handling Ethnically-Biased Situations

If your children complain about a teacher's racially-biased comment or attitude, try to understand what happened and try to avoid passing judgment right away.

Think for a moment about your own prejudices and make space for the possibility that the teacher made a mistake. Ask your children to make an appointment with the teacher where they should explain that the comments or the attitude are making them feel uncomfortable. Suggest that they speak in the first person—"I feel put down when you make these comments"—so that they simply express their feelings and the teacher doesn't feel attacked. Sometimes, just having this meeting will resolve the problem. However, your children may need to talk to the counselor and ask for advice or—if things don't get better—for intervention. If needed, the next step of this process should be a meeting between you, the teacher, the counselor and your child. If the situation doesn't improve, you may want to consider speaking to the principal of the school.

Throughout the situation, keep calm. The more rational you are, the better you are able to explain the situation from your child's point of view—and maybe even clarify some cultural stereotype—and the better your chances of resolving the situation with little negative impact on everyone involved.

Expert to Parent

Dr. Carlisle strongly suggests that parents shop for schools. "I believe Latino parents are not as used to shopping for a school as other groups are. Throughout my career as a superintendent in districts across the country, I always had parents drop by unannounced at my district and ask for a tour of any one of my schools. I knew they were shopping and I did the same thing when I moved from Texas to the Northeast. I went around shopping for schools for my kids."

Identifying and Supporting Your Child's Vocation

High school is also a good time for you and your children to begin exploring their vocations. By now, you probably know what their talents are. Begin discussing what they would like to study when they finish school. Although their ideas may differ from what you want them to study, be open. Youngsters who get pressured to follow a certain career—to support the family business for example, or something that is prestigious in your country—tend to rebel by refusing to go to college. Try to understand that a career is something your children will have to live with for the rest of their lives. It should be their choice.

Having said that, you can guide your children in the process of finding a career that fits their needs and talents. A career in art, for example, does not necessarily mean they will starve. You can help them explore interesting artistic careers that will both allow them to express their talents and support themselves. Talk to the career counselor in school for ideas, visit a career center at the local community college, or conduct Internet searches with your children.

In the United States, people's vocations are highly valued. In a competitive market such as this, it is very important for your children to choose a career where they feel the drive to grow and compete. If you force them to follow the career of *your* dreams, or what is valued in your country, it is very possible that they will not reach their full potential, and they will be unhappy.

Think about it this way—there are probably many aspects of the Latino culture that are a priority to you, like your language, your family values, your religion, etc. These are the aspects you feel that your children must keep alive. Try making sure that your kids carry on these traditions while at the same time realize that in order for them to have better chances to succeed in America you will have to lose some battles. One of them may be the vocation battle. Letting young people choose what they wish to do with their careers is an American trait you may need to embrace.

Most schools offer career exploration courses, but even if your child's school doesn't, it is very likely that it has career programs in its software library that your child can use. Your children can do their own exploration and then discuss their results with you, the guidance or career counselor at school, or another adult who can mentor them. Some of the available programs are: Coin, Choices, and Discover.

They may also want to take a look at the Occupational Outlook Handbook (**www.bls.gov/oco**), a directory published by the federal government that lists every single job out there along with their requirements, their pay scale, and future projections.

Inspirational Capsule

"I strongly think that at times we are our own worst enemies by not pushing ourselves to the next level. Do not dwell in the past or think that you cannot change. Instead, challenge yourself to be your best everyday and focus on the future. Everyday tell yourself a positive affirmation: 'I'm a successful student and I will go to college and graduate next year,'" says María D. Soldevilla.

Chapter 6

How to Help Your Child Stay in School and Out of Trouble

In the last few years, statistics have shown that more and more Latino kids drop out of school—or sometimes they never enter school if they are recent immigrants—to join a gang. The fast growth of urban gangs is worrying authorities and parents alike.

Confronted with a lack of sense of community and belonging, young people look for an alternative that can end up being a very bad choice. This is also an increased risk for children who grew up separated from their parents and join them in the U.S. after many years.

Teacher to Parent

Marjorie Venegas, an ESL teacher who works both at a high school and in a county jail shares: "One way to discover that your child is getting into trouble is by checking the nail of their pinky finger. If it's long and sharp it can be used to snort cocaine and as a weapon to hurt somebody. I teach English in a jail and many of my students have actually killed with that fingernail. You should also check the way they dress. If they used to dress with different colors and now they only wear black or one specific color, it might mean they have joined a gang and those are the gang's colors. Some boys may start wearing eye makeup or earrings, or they may listen to music with very violent lyrics. Some children who used to talk a lot suddenly don't talk or if they used to be very sociable, they suddenly don't go out or go out at odd times, they start failing in school. You have to remain watchful because there are gangs everywhere, not just in the large cities, but in small suburbs too."

How do you make sure your children do not get involved with the wrong people? For starters, you must talk to them and learn to listen to them. Talk to them when they are young, and never stop communicating. Always try to find out about their interests, their concerns, their dreams, and their fears. Make them feel loved, important, and worthy. Be aware that one of the reasons children join gangs is to "be someone." Do not give them the chance to need to be someone in a dangerous environment. Help them reach their best potential by staying in school.

To find out information about different Latino gangs, how and where they operate, their colors, names and specific tattoos they wear, visit The National Alliance of Gangs Investigators' Association (**www.nagia.org**).

Obviously, the best way to help your teenagers stay in school is by staying involved with their education. Again, do not think that because they want their independence, you should back off completely and ignore what is happening in school and in their lives. Teenagers need to be supervised. If you can't be home when they get out of school, make sure they sign up for after school programs. You need to know where they are and with whom at all times.

Parent to Parent

Jorgelina and Fermín Acosta are parents of two teenagers. The older teen, Jocelyn, is studying biology at the University at Buffalo. Jorgelina and Fermín share the secret of their success. As parents with limited education and resources, they managed to encourage their daughter to get involved with the community, have excellent grades and receive scholarships that recognize her academic achievement. "You have to be there every day when children return from school. They should never be left alone to hang out in the streets," Jorgelina says. "We always told them that they had to finish their obligations before they could go outside and play," adds Fermín. "Sometimes kids lie and tell you that they don't have homework so they can go have fun, but we checked every day to see if they had something to do and when they were younger we signed off the homework workbook as well."

As Jocelyn's parents smartly point out, it is essential for you to either be home when the kids come back from school or for you to enroll them in after school programs. The secret is to supervise teenagers so that they are not hanging out with other teenagers alone during all their free time.

You should also take into consideration that children who attended several years of school in Latin America tend to have a hard time adapting to what is usually a faster-paced system. This is a school system where teaching is less personal than in their native countries where teachers know each student personally and treat them as if they were their own kids. As Ms. Venegas points out: "Here, there are thirty to forty students per class and teachers need to do a roll call in order to remember each students' name." If, on top of it, they don't speak English, you can understand why they may feel quite lost in school. Although they will get extra help on the different subjects—usually a second teacher in the classroom will work with them—they will need all the support at home that you can give them to make the transition a little easier.

We all know how challenging adolescents can be. Try to not take things personally, though. If all of a sudden your child doesn't talk to you as much as he or she used to, don't assume immediately it is because there is something wrong with the relationship. Respect their new need for privacy. They are developing their own identity and part of the process is to assert their independence. The key here is to find the balance between supervising them and allowing them a certain level of independence.

Through these difficult years kids deal with a lot of psychological and physical changes, peer pressure, and emotional ups and downs. It is important as a parent that you show them your strength and support, and most of all that you love them and are interested in their well-being.

Things You Can Do to Help Your Child Stay out of Trouble: The Checklist

There are many things you can do to increase the chances of your children staying in school and doing well in their studies, while at the same time, staying out of trouble.

❏ Look for smaller schools where instruction is more personalized. This will help your children feel supported and challenged.

❏ Look for schools where a second language and Latino culture are valued and considered pluses and where they will not be teased or, worse, discriminated against.

❏ Beware of your children's strengths and weaknesses in each subject early on, so you can get them the help they need.

❏ Beware of test dates and preparation requirements.

❏ Make your house the place where your children hang out with friends. This way, you will meet your children's friends and you will be able to better control where your children are and how they spend their time. To accomplish this, suggest that they invite their friends to watch sport games at your house, organize little parties, informal dinners and weekend get-togethers where you welcome your children's friends and maybe even their parents.

❏ Participate in school fairs, fundraisers, and so on, just as you would with your younger children. When your kids see you around school all the time, they know you can easily talk to any of their teachers.

❏ Make it a habit of going to school and finding out your children's attendance, behavior, and grades, even when the school doesn't call you. The teacher may tell you that your children are too quiet or that they do not have friends. This may indicate that there is something happening that you may not have noticed at home.

❏ Establish strict rules and limits. Although they rebel against them, teenagers need and want limits. It shows them that you care about them. For example, many teenagers stay up until very late at night and do not get enough sleep. This affects their school attendance and grades. So, you should limit the amount of time they spend watching television, text messaging, chatting on the Internet, playing video games or talking on the phone.

❏ Use things that give your children pleasure as an incentive when they achieve certain goals. For example, allow them to spend time with their friends in the evening if they prepare for a test and ace it. Take away these privileges if they don't perform as expected.

❏ Try to keep a balance between being your children's friend and being their parent. Parents who are just friends of their kids have a hard time parenting them.

❏ Make sure there is someone home when they return from school or that they are enrolled in extracurricular activities which keep them busy.

Student to Parent

Rodolfo Vaupel, Jr., a 20-year-old sophomore in college, shares: "The wrong people were just other students who gave up due to the barriers in the system. I have seen many kids like me and better go into gangs, drugs, and prostitution due to the barriers they faced to go to college. I stayed in school because my parents told me to just finish high school and see what I would get if I gave it my all. If it weren't for my parents pushing me I would have never even applied to college."

The best way to help your children stay in school, however, is to catch any signs of trouble early on. Doing that requires close attention on your part and a willingness to modify some of your own behavior whenever necessary.

For starters, you should always observe any changes in your children's behavior—for example, they don't pick up their cell phone when you call them, they answer in a bad manner when you ask something, how they dress, their eating habits, and their sleep patterns. The key to your observation is that you should avoid any criticism. When you criticize children, you push them away. They will implement their changes without you knowing about them. For instance, they may leave the expensive clothes they bought with drug money at a friend's house, and you will never find out about it.

So, if you see any changes, ask your children questions like, "Are you making a statement wearing a bandanna?" or "Do you feel you have to wear those baggy pants because the other kids wear them?" There is a big chance that some of the changes with which your children are experimenting have to do with their age, and not with the fact that they have joined a gang or gotten into trouble.

The same is true if your children's grades begin to drop. Explore the cause instead of criticizing or punishing them. Ask questions, such as, "Do you think you need help in this area?" or "Are you getting enough sleep?" "I know you can do better, is there something bothering you?"

Many times criticism takes the form of comments, such as "I don't know who you take after! You have nothing in common with me/this family" or "Your grandfather would be so embarrassed by your behavior." Comments like these may make your children feel that they do not belong in the family and are more likely to push them in the wrong direction. Instead, your goal is to show concern and to provide a welcoming environment so they feel they can talk to you.

Many experts suggest that you organize fun outings with your family. Find out what your children enjoy and do it as a family. That way, they don't feel that they can only have fun with people outside the family.

Another area where you might need to modify your own behavior in order to handle teenagers growing up in the United States is in allowing them to have social time outside of school. Many teenagers feel that they have no time to hang out with their friends outside of school. If you fail to help them build time in their schedule, they will cut classes and eventually drop out.

After establishing clear rules, you also need to allow time and privacy for your children to communicate with their friends.

Parent to Parent

Ricardo Anzaldúa, father of two children who recently graduated from Yale University, suggests that even if parents don't have a lot of success to show for their efforts, they need to find a way to show their children that hard work and dedication will bear fruit. "Parents shouldn't be afraid to tell their kids about their own struggles to get ahead, even if it means talking about deprivation and the poverty in their countries. Many do this out of pride, or to protect their children from the fear of poverty, but the result is that the children don't know the sacrifices their parents made in order to give the children their relatively comfortable lives."

Chapter 7

Parents Who Have Been Separated from Their Children

If you came to the U.S. first and brought your children a few years later, there may be many factors at play that you need to consider carefully. Your children may have a stronger bond with the person who was left in charge of raising them than with you. They may have feelings of abandonment and anger. It's important that you don't try to push too hard for them to love you. Instead, love them and be there for them during this difficult process while you develop a relationship.

Try to help them figure out how school works because they have to deal with many things at the same time—a sense of loss (remember that they left behind their friends, boyfriends or girlfriends, family members, school), a new language, a new culture, and a new family.

> ### Expert to Parent
>
> Anthony Bellettieri, the school psychologist, suggests: "Get as much involved with their work and their lives as you can. When your child comes back from school say something like, 'Let's look at your homework together.' Invite them to go shopping or do other activities. You also need to make your children aware of the reasons you had to make the decisions you made. They need to understand that everything was done for their benefit."

Many times, under these circumstances, it is very difficult for children to respect parents who were not around during the past few years. You need to find a way to communicate with them that recognizes the reality of the situation. As Mr. Belletieri suggests, the best route may be to share with them the reasons you had for coming to the U.S. without them, like finding a job, obtaining legal residency before bringing them along, buying a house, etc. Go over the great sacrifices that you had to make, how hard you worked, how much you suffered by being away from them just so that they could arrive and have an easier time in their new country. Recognize that it was very hard for them, as well; sympathize with their pain and how much they missed you and how much they may now miss the people they left behind.

This process is hard for many parents because they feel that they made such a big effort to bring their children to the U.S. and now their kids are giving them a hard time. Leila Rey, a social worker and educator at the Chicago Public Schools, told me the story of a mother who left her 12-year-old son in Honduras until he was 16. She came to the country alone but later married a man and had three children with him. The teenager, who was dreaming of moving here to live with his mother, suddenly faced a new reality. She was too busy with her new family to pay much attention to him. "He had no projects for his future, he had no motivation; he said his mother was not the same. He judged her not only for having left him behind with his grandmother but because she raised a new family here," Leila shares. "He began to use and sell drugs and when his mother found out, he attempted suicide. On the other hand, the mother feels that this child is a burden on her."

If you had more children when you came to the U.S. while your older children were left in your home country, it's very likely that your teenagers will experience feelings of jealousy towards the younger ones who never had to grow up without you, just as the child in Leila's story did. Be careful with this dynamic.

Student to Parent

"I recommend that you keep track of your kid but do not pressure him or her. Treat the problems you are facing with calm and intelligence. Violence will not resolve anything," suggests Eduardo A. García, 11th-grader at Austin High School, in El Paso, Texas.

When kids arrive in this country as older children or teenagers, it is normal for them to feel disoriented in school. "Middle schools and high schools are very *clique* oriented," explains Mr. Belletieri, "and they are coming in when everyone already belongs to a group. It's hard to enter one of these groups, so these kids often become loners. This is one of the social problems they face. They also tend to gravitate towards kids who are closer to their cultural roots, kids who are not Americanized and unfortunately, some times they will feel closer to kids in an ethnic gang."

These teenagers may also feel that school is a waste of time and that they can do much better finding a job. Or maybe you need them to find a job to help you. If this is the case, try to make arrangements for them to work a certain number of hours and to continue their education either at night school or on the Internet. Find out more information under Other Ways to Fulfill High School Requirements in Chapter 2: The Basics.

There are also cases where one parent, usually the father, goes back to his home country for long periods of time during the year leaving his kids at home with the mother. If this is the case in your family, make sure that the father stays in constant telephone and email communication with your children to minimize the impact that these long absences have on the kids. Teachers, guidance counselors and school psychologists all notice a change in students' behavior and perform-ance during these separation periods.

What is important is that you are aware at all times that your children need you and your support even more than children who grew up here or arrived in the country with you. Besides staying alert and in constant communication with the teachers and guidance coun-selors, you need to seek professional help.

Therapy is a real stigma in the Latino community and that stigma does a real disservice to our families. Try to keep an open mind and realize that providing your children with therapy when they need it may be the best thing you can do to ensure their future success.

Expert to Parent

"Many Latino kids have lost their respect for their elders, their parents, their grandparents, authorities... They think they can treat anyone like they treat their friends. You even see it in students who have just arrived and within three months they are not submissive any more, many have changed their physical appearance. They are obviously looking for attention. Parents need to be very involved in these kids' schools to show them that they care, and that they can drop by at any time and talk to any teacher. They should be part of the PTA and be around all the time," shares Marjorie Venegas, ESL teacher.

One last word on this issue. If you still have children in your home country and you are working on bringing them over, Robin Bikkal, the immigration lawyer, suggests that you may want to travel back and forth to your country a few times to establish a rapport and a good measure of respect with your children before you bring them over. Once you establish a relationship with them and a sense of authority, you will all have an easier time adjusting to the new situation of them living with you in the U.S.

Chapter 8

Options for Postsecondary Education

Before your children can decide what they want to do regarding their education after high school, it's important to understand the options available. First you need to know that colleges may be public or private. Public colleges are less expensive and are supported by state funds. Tuition for students who live in the state is much cheaper than for students who live out of state. Private colleges are supported by tuition and money from donors. Although they are more expensive than public colleges, they can offer scholarships and financial aid to be more affordable to students who may need help.

Expert to Parent

Dr. Jorge Castellanos, chairperson of the Spanish department and director of the Latin American Studies Program at Manhattanville College says: "The advantage of attending a smaller college, like Manhattanville, is that it provides a warmer, nurturing, student-centered environment. Both students and faculty benefit from a deeply caring, diverse community that

> encourages student leadership. In addition, as a result of a lower teacher to student ratio, everyone knows each other on a more personal level. This environment supports a genuine understanding of a curriculum that promotes academic, social and personal success."

Universities

Universities are usually larger than colleges and may actually have different schools or colleges within them—business school, law school, etc. Some universities award doctorates, and they tend to have research facilities and a wide variety of social opportunities, like fraternities, sororities, clubs, etc. They can be private or public. The top eight universities in the country are part of what is known as the Ivy League. They include: Brown University, Columbia University, Cornell University, Dartmouth College, Harvard University, Princeton University, University of Pennsylvania, and Yale University. These are some of the very best universities in the country and there are many advantages to attending them—they not only attract some of the best faculty and best programs and have the best reputation, but they also offer a fantastic network. Once your children graduate from one of these universities, they have access to the alumni of the school who is always ready to lend a hand to graduates of their alma matter.

These connections are pivotal for career advancement and for all sorts of other advantages. If your child is a really good student, explore the scholarships available to attend the top schools in the country. In an effort to attract more diversity, they are also offering interesting financial aid packages to the right candidates.

Colleges

Generally speaking, colleges tend to be smaller than universities and they can also be private or public. There are two year colleges and four year colleges; there are some which offer only *bachelor's degrees* (undergraduate degree) and others that offer graduate degrees. It all depends on the individual school.

Community Colleges/Junior Colleges

When it comes to their Latino students, many guidance counselors tend to recommend they attend *community colleges* (public and nonresidential) or *junior colleges* (private schools where the students live on campus or in the surrounding community) that are colleges that offer *associate's degrees* (two-year degrees). Sometimes the fact that these counselors don't encourage students to apply to the best four-year schools is a combination of misinformation and the cultural stereotype (based in reality!) that Latino parents don't want their kids to go away to college.

Community college is a great alternative given the right circumstance. For example:

- Students who wish to further their education and for whom money is an issue and they don't have the grades to qualify for scholarships.

- Students who don't have good grades or a good SAT or ACT score and want to clean up their act before applying to more demanding schools.

- Students who have a family situation—maybe a relative who needs care—that forces them to stay at home.

Again, under the right circumstances even the top tier schools will be happy to consider students who went to a community college. It all boils down to your children being able to explain why they took certain educational steps along the way.

In this country, community colleges have made education possible for thousands of people who are now very successful. Because the admission requirements are less stringent than in four year colleges, many students get their associate's degree first and then they transfer to a four year school to get their bachelor's. If this is the plan, your children should be sure to take courses that can later be transferred.

What is important for you and your children to do before you decide that community college is the way to go, is to evaluate all the options at your child's disposal. Evaluate the real chances of getting into the best schools, study the scholarships and financial aid that they could receive, and project the type of career paths that one school would offer over the next. Don't make your decisions based only on the fact that the community college is around the corner and it's cheaper. Don't let your own desire to keep your children living at home, limit your children's opportunities of success in this country. Becoming independent is one of the biggest lessons your children can learn.

Inspirational Capsule

"Living away from home is hard. I miss my mom's cooking and the fact that for my birthday she makes spaghetti for me. And today is my birthday and I'm here in school. But I think living alone has taught me a lot of responsibility and I'm grateful for that," shares Jocelyn Acosta, who is studying biology at Buffalo University and whose family lives 300 miles away.

When doing research on colleges, remind your children to verify that the school they wish to attend is accredited by one of the following regional accrediting organizations:

- Middle States Association of Colleges and Schools Middle States Commission on Higher Education

- New England Association of Schools and Colleges Commission on Institutions of Higher Education

- New England Association of Schools and Colleges Commission on Technical and Career Institutions

- North Central Association of Colleges and Schools the Higher Learning Commission

- Northwest Commission on Colleges and Universities

- Southern Association of Colleges and Schools Commission on Colleges

- Western Association of Schools and Colleges Accrediting Commission for Community and Junior Colleges

- Western Association of Schools and Colleges Accrediting Commission for Senior Colleges and Universities

Technical/Vocational Schools

These types of schools place emphasis on specific careers such as computer technology, culinary arts, real estate, automotive, etc. There are some schools that offer one specific trade while others offer several. You can find a comprehensive list of these schools at **www.khake.com**. Some of these schools offer correspondence courses that your kids can take online. Depending on the school, they offer licenses, certificates, and a varying range of degrees. Receiving an accreditation from these schools will generally enable students to get employed at their trade. They may or may not be able to transfer credits to the more traditional degree programs, so they should find out this information before they make a decision to attend.

Expert to Parent

Martita Mestey, senior vice president of Strategic Partnerships at iHispano (**www.ihispano.com**), an online job search engine, shares her experience as a recruiter: "If students are thinking of getting an MBA for example, no employer is going to look at what school they went to for their four year college. The moment they get the MBA, that undergraduate degree becomes obsolete. Employers want to know where you got your MBA. So, it's better to save money and go to a less expensive four year college and then go to a really good, even if it's very expensive, graduate school. Some people get it backwards. They spend a lot of money on their undergraduate degree and then they can't afford the MBA. There is no way around it: a good school breeds more opportunities."

Chapter 9

What Colleges Look for in an Applicant

High school is a very important part of children's education, regardless of whether they will continue on to college or look for a job. The skills they will acquire during these four years will help them do better in life in general. That is why you should encourage them to work hard and to have some fun at the same time. Patricia Garrity, the principal of Cristo Rey Jesuit High School says that her students "absolutely love coming to school. It's a privilege to work in a place like this, where students love to come and so do teachers." This is important because if high school is a positive experience for your teenagers, they will be encouraged to continue their studies. As I said throughout these pages, it is also crucial that you help them keep an eye on the bigger prize: their college degree. Even in schools that are not in the top tier, admission is very competitive. That is the reason why it is essential that during their high school years students focus on what colleges look for in an applicant so they can build up their high school resume in a consistent way.

Amongst the many people I interviewed for this book and for this chapter in particular, Chioma Isiadinso, the CEO of Expartus (**www.expartus.com**), a company that helps parents and students understand the fundamentals of admission to top schools, has a lot of important points to share. In addition to her consulting experience, Chioma was the assistant director of admissions at Harvard Business School and the director of admissions at Carnegie Mellon School of Public Policy. This is a woman who knows the thinking of admissions officers inside out! In this section, you will hear her suggestions often.

Good Grades

Having good grades is very important to colleges. As you and your children begin your research, you will find out that many colleges have a minimum GPA requirement. That's why it is so essential for your children to have good grades from 9th grade on. Understanding early-on how the grading system works in this country, will help them stay focused on the hard work involved in getting A's. Remind them that this kind of commitment to schoolwork needs to continue until graduation. Sometimes seniors feel that they can slack off but many colleges have revoked their offers to students who have shown that tendency. However, even if your children begin their high school career with weak grades, it's never too late to turn things around as colleges look at whether grades improved over time. This means that someone who had low grades in 9th and 10th grades but improved in 11th and continued to improve in 12th grade can be seen in a very positive light.

A Challenging Course Load

Admissions officers look for students who choose to challenge themselves. They prefer students who take honors classes and advanced placement courses over those who take standard courses. So, your job is to look at the course offerings with your children and to encourage them to choose the harder ones. Even if they get a B average, it's very likely that a college will choose them over a student with an A average who only took standard courses. If your children only take standard courses they make it easy for the admissions officers to turn them down. Basically, colleges are looking for students who show that they have it in them to challenge themselves and to push forward in the face of tough classes.

Good SAT and ACT Scores

The scores on your children's SAT and ACT tests are an important determining factor in the college admissions process. Chioma Isiadinso suggests that students prepare and take the PSAT in 10th grade to assess where they may need help. That year they need to prepare for the SAT and ACT so they can take it during the first semester of 11th grade. "This way, if they don't do well, they have time to take it again while they are still in 11th grade. The key is to avoid waiting until 12th grade to take the SAT/ACT because then there's nothing they can do to improve their score." Ms. Isiadinso also reveals that students who get almost perfect scores on their SAT or ACT have been preparing with coaches for a long time. Although these classes can be costly, there are some nonprofit organizations that offer them for free. For example, *Let's Get Ready* **www.letsgetready.org** is a network of students run college access programs. The organization's volunteers serve as coaches, mentors and role models who guide underserved students on their path to fulfill their college dreams. They provide intensive SAT and college preparation courses three times a year. Check their website for locations. Also, talk to your children's guidance counselor to find out about local organizations that offer free SAT and ACT preparation.

Extracurricular Activities

As we discussed in Chapter 4: Extracurricular Activities and Summer Programs, being involved in extracurricular activities is a wonderful asset for college admission. "It used to be that admission officers were looking for well-rounded people who did all sorts of things. Most recently, it is about being passionate about something and having a focus early-on in 9th and 10th grades," recommends Ms. Isiadinso. The idea is for your children to choose something they are passionate about and get involved with it consistently.

Expert to Parent

"If your child likes chess, for example, he can become the president of the chess club. If there is no chess club in his or her high school, he can create one. Then, maybe he or she will start a chess competition to help raise funds to help inner city schools. This shows his or her passion and his or her social responsibility, an attitude towards helping others who are less fortunate," explains Chioma Isiadinso.

Pursuing summer programs that are consistent with their passion is another asset at the time of applying to college, so review that chapter carefully. Given the number of scholarships available (check Chapter 10), when the time comes, you can't use the excuse that you couldn't afford these activities. Once you and your children identify their passion, research available programs and funds so that they can pursue it.

The other key aspect of getting involved in extracurricular activities is for students to take on leadership roles. This will not only give them visibility in the school or the community, but it will help them develop many useful skills for later in life. And that is exactly what colleges are most interested in—students who have demonstrated leadership skills. Once again, it's better for students to pick a few activities on which they can focus, to which they can devote time and energy, and in which they can stand out, than to select too many, just to make their high school resume look good.

College Application Essay

Just as with the scholarships, the college application requires that your children write an essay. There will be a description of the type of essay the college is looking for on the application. Usually, they want a personal statement or a situation experienced by the student which shows what he or she is all about, or what things are important to him or her. This is the perfect opportunity for your children to express their dreams, their objectives, any particular events that contributed to shaping them into who they are and anything about their family and culture that motivates them to move forward. It is also a chance to talk about how the experience they gained doing their extracurricular activities ties in with their future plans. They should tell their story in a way that highlights their determination, their ability to overcome obstacles, their interest for helping others, and so on.

Expert to Parent

"Admissions people don't like students who hide behind their circumstances. If someone has a horrible personal story, they want to see how they raised above it and still made it through high school. They love to see redemption stories. I remember when I worked in admissions at Harvard, there was a young lady who had lost her parents and had been homeless for two years during high school. She still managed to stay in school and keep her grades. She went to MIT and then came to Harvard. So, she did have an awful story, but she didn't let that stop her," shares Chioma Isiadinso.

You need to know that there is a process for writing a good essay and that there are many websites where your children can review samples from students who were admitted to top universities. On these sites they can also get tips on writing a winning essay. One example is **www.collegeboard.com**.

Other websites offer editors who will not only brainstorm the topic for the essay with your children, but they will also critique it and edit it for an affordable fee. Some good resources are **www.essayedge.com** and **www.quintcareers.com**. If your child decides not to use any of these services, make sure he or she has the essay reviewed by someone who has a very good command of English, preferably an advanced college student or professor.

Letters of Recommendation

Part of the college application process involves getting two or three letters of recommendation from people who know your child. Some colleges require a specific teacher while others let students choose. Usually the junior or senior year math or English teacher—if they know your child well enough—and the guidance counselor are good candidates. The key here is for your child to ask teachers who know his or her academic achievements as well as his or her involvement with other activities so they can write a strong recommendation. Remind your child to ask for the letters of recommendation early to give teachers at least a month before the deadline. Then, make sure they check with the writers to see if they sent the letters in, at least a week prior to the deadline. Also, whenever appropriate, your child should waive his or her right to review the recommendation as this gives more credibility to it.

The Interview

Most colleges will give your child the chance to request an interview. This is a face to face meeting with an admissions officer where students get to tell their story; where they get to share things that usually can not be conveyed on the fifty word statement that is part of the application. The goal of this interview is to make the admissions officer feel comfortable with the applicant as a prospective student of that particular college.

For Chioma Isiadinso the interview is an ideal tool for students with a non-traditional situation. So, for instance, if your child is 22 years old and is only now graduating, the interview would afford him or her a unique environment to explain his or her story. "Officers would love to hear that your child had to help with the family business for a couple of years. It shows his determination, his resiliency, his commitment to help others," says Isiadinso. Other examples of situations that may need an explanation include any gap in your child's high school resume, a sudden drop in grades—it may be due to an illness or the fact that he or she had to take care of a sick relative—a departure from the basketball team after years of commitment, etc.

The interview is also a good opportunity for youngsters with a great personality and who are very articulate to shine and gain a competitive advantage over other students with identical qualifications.

Diversity and Other Important Factors

One very important point to keep in mind when applying to college is the fact that your children are of Latino descent. Many colleges are actively trying to recruit good Latino students because they are not well represented in their campuses. They will look closely at applicants with a diverse background. While there are usually no formal quotas, it is crucial for minority students to talk about what they bring to the particular college to which they are applying and how they will enrich the student body. This perspective can be particularly interesting to the admissions officer and give your child an edge over other candidates.

A diversity of socioeconomic backgrounds is also something universities look for. For example, for some colleges it may be important to have a group of first generation college students on campus, or students from the migrant community. There are even some private colleges that offer huge financial aid packages to students from middle and low income families. This means that if you think you can't afford to send your child to a great private university, contact the school, find out if they offer financial aid to Latinos, and then visit the scholarship websites listed on Chapter 10.

Early Action or Early Decision

If your child knows early on what college he or she wishes to attend, it may be a good idea to consider applying early. There are two options for early application: early action and early decision.

Early Action

This means that the student applies early and gets an early answer. Usually, students apply by November 1, and they receive their answers by the middle of December. The advantage is that students find out sooner that they have been admitted to college and they can enjoy the last few months of high school without having to worry. Applying and being accepted through early action doesn't mean that your child has to attend the college where he or she was accepted. He or she has the opportunity to apply to as many schools via the early action program as he or she wishes and then compare the different financial aid packages offered from various colleges in order to choose the best option.

Early Decision

Generally speaking it follows the same idea as early action: your child applies early, usually by November 1, and gets an answer by mid-December. There is a big difference between the two programs, though. Early decision plans are binding, which means that if your child applies to a college via this process, he or she will have to attend this particular college if he or she gets accepted. This also means that he or she can only apply to one early decision school. He or she can, however, apply to as many colleges under regular admission as he or she wishes. But, if your child gets accepted at the early decision school, he or she must withdraw all the other applications.

The advantage of early decision is that colleges tend to offer students better possibilities of being admitted if they apply early. In early decision colleges, the acceptance rates of students who apply early are better than for students who apply via regular admission. The problem with early decision is that your child may be accepted before his or her financial packages have been awarded in which case he or she may not know if he or she can afford the school.

My suggestion is that unless your children don't need the rest of their senior year to improve their grades or their high school resume and you are sure you can afford the early admission school, encourage your children to apply through the regular admissions process. Either way, your children should discuss these options with their guidance counselor.

Secrets of Getting an Acceptance Letter from College: The Checklist

❏ Help your children think about college early so they can direct their high school efforts towards their goal.

❏ Help your children identify their passion early on and help them find ways to channel that passion through extracurricular activities. Motivate them to seek leadership roles in whatever they get involved.

❏ Make sure your children are consistent with their extracurricular and volunteer activities and don't jump from one program to the next.

❏ Encourage your teenagers to study hard and pick honors courses. Someone with a B average who took more demanding courses will do better than someone with an A average who only took standard courses.

❏ Insist that your children spend time preparing for the SAT and ACT. Explore available preparation courses in your area.

❏ Given the right circumstances, pursuing a high school diploma online or taking some courses online may be the greatest decision for your children.

Inspirational Capsule

Alex DeLeon, a student at Columbia University, says that being in college "is fun and challenging. It's very different from living at home where you are kept to one world. Leaving away from home opens your mind to different views, so it's really important to live away."

Chapter 10

Paying for College

When asked whether they are planning to attend college, many students answer that their parents can't afford it, which is a shame given that there is so much money available! Millions of dollars go unused every year because people don't know that it's there.

So, before you tell your child that you can't pay for his or her college, read this section very carefully; you will find great information about grants that you don't have to repay, student loans and how you can save for college.

Student to Parent

"I come from a poor family. They couldn't pay for college because it's too expensive, so I looked for scholarships. I got the HACER scholarship from the Ronald McDonald House Charities and a scholarship from the University at Buffalo where I'm studying biology. My suggestion for students is to manage their time because everything happens at once. I basically dedicated one weekend to each activity. One to fill out the FAFSA, one to fill out the CSA profile, one for the scholarships... Sometimes it's hard because you want to go out and have fun with your friends, but four weekends of your life is absolutely nothing," shares Jocelyn Acosta, a student at University at Buffalo.

Financial Aid

A long time before your children begin applying to colleges, you must have a conversation about your family's financial situation to assess how much you will be able to pay for school, and how much you will need to get from different sources. A great tool to help in calculating the cost of your child's education is the Tuition Cost Calculator at **www.princetonreview.com**. This will give you an idea of how much financial aid you will need. Cost, however, should not be the underlying factor in choosing the right college. In this country, there are many forms of financial aid—grants, scholarships, work-study, and loans—available to students from low-income families. But no matter what your child's financial situation is, he or she should apply for financial aid. To become eligible for federal financial aid or a Pell Grant, your children must submit a *Free Application for Federal Student Aid* (FAFSA). The FAFSA can be found at the guidance counselor's office, local public library, college financial aid office, the FAFSA website (**www.fafsa.ed.gov**), or by calling the Federal Student Aid Information Center (FSAIC) at 1-800-4-FED-AID. The FAFSA is also available in Spanish.

Financial aid makes up the difference between what you can afford to pay and what the college costs. Aid is offered by the federal government and individual universities or colleges. There are three types of financial aid: grants and scholarships, loans, and work-study. Grants and scholarships do not have to be repaid. However, grants are offered based on financial need, whereas scholarships are awarded based on merit. Loans, on the other hand, must be repaid. Most federal education loan programs offer lower interest rates and flexible repayment plans. The third type of aid comes in the form of work-study or student employment. It helps students pay for education costs such as, textbooks, supplies, and personal expenses.

Before filling out the FAFSA, you should gather all the documents and other information needed to complete the application. The FAFSA application requires both your child's and your own financial information. Your child must submit the FAFSA every year that he or she wants to receive aid. Be sure he or she submits the application before the deadline. This will ensure that it is processed in time for the upcoming school year. For a list of documents your child will need in order to complete the FAFSA check out Student Aid on the Web: **www.student.ed.gov**. On this website he or she will also find individual descriptions for the questions he or she will be required to answer in the application, and information concerning deadlines. This can be an overwhelming process for your children to carry out on their own. So once again, let me encourage you to either be a part of it or find another adult or college student who can be by their side.

The majority of financial aid requires the student to be a United States citizen, permanent resident, or eligible non-citizen. Aid is not generally available to undocumented students, but some states do allow these students to qualify for in-state tuition rates. If your child is a United States citizen, but one or more parents are undocumented, he or she is still eligible for financial aid.

For more information about Federal Student Financial Aid call the Federal Student Aid Information Center (FSAIC) and request a free copy of The Student Guide: Financial Aid from the U.S. Department of Education.

Here are some websites that offer information about the FAFSA and other types of aid available:

- **www.finaid.org**

- **www.collegeboard.com**

- **www.mapping-your-future.org**

- **www.collegeispossible.org**

- **www.princetonreview.com**

Scholarships

When we talk about scholarships, there is a wide variety of them. There are scholarships for undergraduate studies and for graduate studies; some are for specific careers; some are national, while others are local. They are sponsored by all kinds of companies, foundations, publications, associations, and even labor unions. Just take a look at the products you and your children use, the associations you belong to, the faith you embrace and you will be surprised by the fact that many of those organizations offer scholarships. The amount varies widely but keep in mind that your child may apply to as many scholarships as he or she wishes. Each scholarship has a slightly different set of requirements so it's important to visit the various websites and study the information carefully. Once you and your child decide on which scholarships he or she should apply for, I suggest that you put them on a calendar so you don't miss any deadlines.

A Word on Requirements

Although each scholarship has a different set of requirements, most of them ask for a minimum GPA—generally 3.0—and that your child is registered to attend college within a certain amount of time of getting the scholarship. Some of them are only available to residents or citizens of the United States, although there are some that don't enforce this requirement—read the information about MALDEF below. Most of them want students who are involved with the community and who show leadership skills. For scholarships that are specifically targeted to Latinos, you will notice that they are particularly interested in students who show leadership in the Latino community. Most of them require an essay of some sort and an application.

Secrets to Obtaining Scholarships

When I talk to people who were successful obtaining scholarships about the secrets of their success, they all seem to agree on a few important areas:

- **Research**

  The only way you can get a scholarship is if you know that it exists. You need to help your children find out what is available to them and then help them through the application process.

- **Well-written Essay**

  Many times, your children may not have the perfect English skills to ace this requirement. If this is the case, try to find someone who can work with them on the essay and who can review it. It can be an English-speaking student who does well in school, a tutor, or a family member with good English skills.

- ■ **Community Involvement**
  Students need to be very involved in the community and show strong leadership skills in the agency or program with which they get involved. Throughout this book I have insisted on the importance of volunteering and getting involved in extra curricular activities. Review that information for ideas you can share with your children.

- ■ **Good Grades**
  It's important that kids pay attention to their grades from ninth grade on!

Most people tend to think that the only determining factor for getting scholarships is having good grades, but the truth is that it is a combination of things. The more elements your child brings to the table, the better the chances of obtaining the coveted prize.

College Graduate to Parent

Gladys Bernett, president of the Tampa Bay Chapter of the National Society of Hispanic MBAs and Vice President Institutional Division, Eagle Asset Management, who has earned a Master in Business Administration and a Master in Health Administration, dispels certain myths about paying for college:

1. As a parent I need to have thousands saved for my children's college education.

Parents should help their children look at those colleges that better fit their academic, career, and professional needs and interests, and should later look into cost issues. Of course cost is important; however, according to the College Board, there are more than $90 billion dollars in financial aid available in scholarships, grants and in low interest financial aid loans.

2. Scholarships are only available to straight-A students.

Although it is true that some aid is based on merit, the majority of the financial aid out there is based on need. There are scholarships and grants with different requirements and for different majors. I had a friend who got a scholarship for her graduate degree because her right eye had two tones, hazel and green. This was an endowment given to the university by someone with the same eye characteristic! There are many scholarships available to a variety of students with different ethnic background or physical characteristics.

3. If my child gets student loans he or she will take forever to pay these off.

According to the Census, college grads on average earn $1 million more over their careers than high school graduates. The more degrees students have under their belts, the more they can increase their earning potential. Even though the debt will be higher, at the end they will be able to repay it quickly as they advance in their careers. Also, even if they have student loans they can still apply for scholarships to supplement the costs.

It's all a question of helping them do the research!!

Some Very Useful Resources

One good place to start your search for scholarships is **www.fastweb.com** where you can search for colleges or scholarships. On this website your child creates a detailed profile which includes personal information, his or her area of interest, geographic area where he or she wants to go to school, specific characteristics such as culture, any disabilities, etc. Using all this data, this search engine comes up with a list of matches. Another good resource is **www.petersons.com**, a website that not only offers information on billions of dollars worth of scholarships for students in the U.S. but also for international students.

You should also check out **www.scholarshipsfor hispanics.org**, the educational arm of the National Association of Hispanic Publishers. They offer a comprehensive list of scholarships available for Latino students and they are making a big outreach effort to get more companies to sponsor grants. They offer their free directory on CD-ROM as well as online. On their website you can search for scholarships that don't require residency or citizenship.

There is a wonderful website where you can find an extensive compilation of scholarships, fellowships, internships, summer programs, post graduate awards and much more compiled by Dr. Francisco Alberto Tomei: **http://scholarships.fatomei.com**.

You and your children can search by area of interest, gender, ethnicity, and a whole number of other options. It even includes grants available for K-12.

Several organizations administer scholarship programs offered by various corporations. For example, the *Hispanic Scholarship Fund* (HSF) **www.hsf.net** is the nation's leading organization supporting Hispanic higher education. It offers scholarships for high school seniors and for college undergraduates and graduates. Among others, it manages the Gates Millennium Scholars Fund that provides substantial awards to students with good academic skills and substantial financial needs. HSF has distributed 25 million dollars in scholarships to Latinos in 2005–2006.

Another such organization is the *Hispanic College Fund* (HCF) **www.hispanicfund.org**, which lists in its website several scholarships offered by corporate sponsors. Their scholarship programs focus on developing Latino youth who are pursuing undergraduate degrees in business, science, engineering, technology, pharmacy, accounting, math, and other specialties. They administer the Sallie Mae scholarship, which offers funding for students who are the first one in their families to go to college. In 2006, HCF awarded 550 scholarships, totaling $2.4 million.

The *Mexican American Legal Defense and Educational Fund* (MALDEF) **www.maldef.org** is a national nonprofit organization whose mission is to protect and promote the civil rights of the Latinos living in the United States. Each year MALDEF awards numerous law school scholarships to students entering their first, second or third year of law school. Scholarships range up to $7,000 per individual. MALDEF has compiled a list of scholarships available to Latino students who are undocumented. You can find the list on their website.

With approximately 115,000 members throughout the United States and Puerto Rico, *LULAC* (**www.lulac.org**) is the largest and oldest Hispanic Organization in the United States. LULAC advances the economic condition, educational attainment, political influence, health and civil rights of Hispanic Americans through community-based programs operating at more than 700 LULAC councils nationwide. The organization involves and serves all Hispanic nationality groups.

Historically, LULAC has focused heavily on education, civil rights, and employment for Hispanics. Its councils provide more than $1 million dollars in scholarships to Hispanic students each year, they conduct citizenship and voter registration drives, develop low income housing units, conduct youth leadership training programs, and seek to empower the Hispanic community at the local, state and national level.

College Student to Parent

"I received several scholarships because of my Hispanic heritage. Columbia University has financial aid based on need so I received many grants from Columbia. I expressed that I am someone who can achieve my goals and I displayed my appreciation for my Hispanic heritage," shares Alex DeLeon, a Columbia University College student.

The Tomás Rivera Policy Institute, funded by The Sallie Mae Fund, the Walt Disney Company, and Southern California Edison, developed a directory of available grants and scholarships offered specifically to California Latino students (**www.latinocollege dollars.org**). Your children can visit the site where they can enter their GPA and look for opportunities. They can search both for scholarships that require citizenship and for ones that don't.

You should also look into private funding sources. A good example of an independent organization that administers its own scholarships is the *Ronald McDonald House Charities* (RMHC). With the support of McDonald's Corporation, the McDonald's Hispanic Owner/Operators Association and the public, RMHC offers the HACER scholarships, specifically targeted to Latinos. In general, the scholarships are offered to high school seniors with an average 3.0 GPA who are legal residents of the U.S.. Students need to prepare a personal statement and demonstrate community involvement. In 2005–2006, RMHC distributed around 1.6 million dollars in HACER scholarships throughout the country. To identify participating RMHC Chapters, find out about the requirements and obtain additional information about the HACER scholarship visit **www.meencanta.com**. Scholarships range between $1,000 and $20,000.

One of the private foundations that issues a large amount of money in scholarships is *The Gates Millennium Scholars* (GMS) (**www.gmsp.org**). Its goal is to provide outstanding African American, American Indian/Alaska Native, Asian Pacific Islander American, and Hispanic American students with an opportunity to complete an undergraduate college education in all discipline areas and a graduate education for those students pursuing studies in mathematics, science, engineering, education, library science, or public health. For more information you can visit their website or Hispanic Scholarship Fund's website.

You also need to be aware of the fact that there are a large number of scholarships available for graduate students. Some are offered by foundations, some by universities, some by private companies and others by the various professional associations like the *National Association of Hispanic Nurses, American Bar Foundation, American Institute of Certified Public Accountants*, etc. Here are two good examples of associations that sponsor scholarships for graduate students:

The *National Society of Hispanic MBAs* (NSHMBA) (**www.nshmba.org**), for example, provides scholarships to students seeking their MBA. Its goal is to foster Hispanic leadership through graduate management education and professional development. The idea is that these leaders can provide the cultural awareness and sensitivity vital in the management of the nation's diverse workforce. It has offered over $1 million dollars in scholarships in 2005–2006.

The *National Association of Hispanic Journalists* (NAHJ) (**www.nahj.org**) offers several scholarships designed to encourage and assist Latino students pursue careers in journalism. As Hispanics remain underrepresented in mainstream U.S. newsrooms, one of NAHJ's goals is to help more qualified Hispanic students to move from the classroom to the newsroom. NAHJ offers scholarships to college undergraduates and graduate students pursuing careers as print, photo, broadcast or online journalism. Their scholarships range between $1,000 and $5,000.

Inspirational Capsule

"I arrived in this country seven years ago with a work visa. My son got excellent grades in school and he was convinced he would get a scholarship to go to college. When the time came, he found out that he didn't qualify for the State of Georgia HOPE scholarship because he wasn't a resident. He wouldn't give up. We took him to several college fairs where he picked up information on the colleges in which he was interested. He wrote letters to each one of these schools explaining his situation and asking for scholarships. He received six positive responses and accepted the one from Wake Forest University in Winston Salem, North Carolina. It's amongst the 30 best universities in the country. They gave him $30,000 for tuition and $11,000 for room and board, so we are not paying a dime for it. His success is a testament of his perseverance. He also showed in his essays his interest in helping other Latinos and in becoming a role model for the community," says Rodolfo Vaupel, President of Vaupel Insurance Agency and 2007 President of the Atlanta Chapter of the National Society of Hispanic MBAs (NSHMBA).

Scholarships for the Wealthy

More and more colleges are offering financial help to wealthy families. The reason is that it helps improve the school's profile in the college rankings, and also, these families can pay a substantial part of their children's education. Another reason is that these students will become future alumni with deep pockets. The caveat is that in order to get some of the money available, your child has to be an above average student.

So, if your income doesn't qualify your child for a financial need based scholarship, keep your focus on merit based scholarships. You can go to: **www.foxcollege funding.com** for information on strategies to apply for college funding. Visit the website of the universities your child is interested in and contact their admissions office to ask about scholarship requirements. You will also find valuable information in the book *The A's and B's of Academic Scholarships*, by Anna Leider, where she lists 100,000 scholarships ranging from $200 to $35,000. *The College Board* (**www.collegeboard.com**) and *Peterson's* (**www.petersons.com**) offer an academic profile of freshmen students at the different schools that includes their average GPA. If your child has a better GPA than the average of the school, he or she may have a chance of getting a merit based scholarship.

Work Study Program

Work-study programs are a form of financial aid in which your children perform work in exchange for money for their education. Federal government programs are the primary source of work-study, but individual states or campuses may also offer their own programs to make additional financial aid available to as many students as possible.

Your children's *Student Aid Report* (SAR—the response they get after completing the FAFSA) is one indicator used by the college in determining their eligibility for the Federal Work-study program. Work-study programs have rules about whether the work can be on-campus—where students work for their own college—or off-campus—where the employer is usually a non-profit organization or a public agency—and the maximum number of hours per week students can work. The program encourages students to do community work and work related to their studies.

The amount your children can earn varies depending on when they apply, their level of financial need, and their school's funding level. If they apply early, they'll have a better chance of receiving federal work-study funds. The campus financial aid officer should have the details specific to your children's program.

Student Loans

There are a number of different loans available to students. Unlike other forms of financial aid, loans must be repaid with interest. Because this is a complex subject, I suggest that you approach someone with an accounting or financial background who can go over the information with you and explain any areas that are not clear to you.

Here's a breakdown of the most important ones you need to explore:

■ Stafford Loans are for undergraduate students, and are made through one of two United States Department of Education programs. The first is the *Direct Stafford Loan* program, and the second is the *Federal Family Education Loan* (FFEL) program— referred to as the Federal Stafford Loan. Direct

Stafford Loan Program funds come directly from the federal government through the United States Department of Education. Funds for the Federal Stafford Loan come from the bank, credit union, or other lenders that participate in the program.

■ Federal Perkins Loans are made through participating schools for undergraduate and graduate students with exceptional financial need and usually have longer repayment plans. Interest does not accumulate while the student is in school.

■ The Federal PLUS Loan Program enables parents, instead of students, to take out a loan for their dependent undergraduate child, but generally must begin payment while the student is in school.

When it comes to federal loans, students must repay them after they graduate, leave school, or drop below full-time enrollment. They are given a *grace period* of six months for Direct Stafford Loans or Federal Family Education Loan (FFEL) and nine months for Federal Perkins loans to begin repayment. Both Direct and Federal Stafford programs offer students four repayment plans, but the Federal Perkins Loan Program offers only one. Students generally have ten years to repay all their loans, there are some variations depending on which plan they choose. Monthly payments will depend on the size of your child's debt and the length of his or her repayment period. To help students keep track of their loans, the United States Department of Education's National Student Loans Data System (NSLDS) allows them to access information on loan and or federal grant amounts, and loan status (including due balances and disbursements).

■ If federal loans do not provide enough money, or a more flexible repayment plan is needed, Private Education Loans are also available. These are granted by private lenders; they are subsidized loans and are granted based on financial need. The federal government will pay the interest on the loan while the student is still in school and for the first six months after the student leaves school.

The difference between a subsidized and an unsubsidized loan is that in the latter case the student is responsible for the interest from the time the unsubsidized loan is disbursed until it is paid in full. Interest rates can vary from year to year. Stafford Loans can be subsidized or unsubsidized because they are funded by the Federal government. The only difference is the amount of interest the student pays. Private Education Loans are funded by private financial institutions. Students do not need to fill out any federal forms to receive a Private Education Loan.

There are many websites dedicated to offering information about loans for students and parents. VOY is an organization that has partnered with Student Loans Corporation to provide borrowers with great customer service and education loan opportunities. Another organization is Sallie Mae which offers information and resources to students and parents about the financial aid process.

For more information:

National Student Loans Data System for Students
www.nslds.ed.gov

VOY
www.voystudentloans.com

Sallie Mae
www.salliemae.com

TERI
www.teri.org

Nelnet
www.nelnet.net

Saving for College

If you have younger kids, the sooner you start saving for college the better. College is very expensive and you will need to save over a long period of time to be able to help your children pay for it. Here are two ways that you can prepare for the future.

To obtain more information on the accounts we discuss in this section and on others that may be available, you can visit **www.savingforcollege.com** or **www.finaid.org**. You should also talk to your local bank manager or financial advisor to receive detailed and professional explanations of these savings plans.

- **529 College Savings Plan.** It's an education savings plan operated by a state or an educational institution. It is designed to help you set funds aside for future college expenses. Almost all states now offer a 529 plan and, under a new law, educational institutions can offer their own plan. These plans are usually categorized as prepaid or savings. You can either prepay a specific college where you wish to send your kids or deposit the money into your state's 529 plan account. You don't need to send your children to a state college even if you have a 529 state plan. When the time comes, you can transfer the funds to any private college. Although the specifics vary from state to state, the deposits and the interest they generate are tax exempt as are the withdrawals you make to pay for education expenses. In most states you can put up to $300,000 per beneficiary into the account. The interesting aspect of this plan is that it gives you all the control over the account; your child is the beneficiary but if he or she decides not to go to college, you can either name a different beneficiary—if you have a younger child who is interested in college, for example—or recover the money for yourself. In this case, a portion of the money will be subject to income tax and a 10% penalty. Find out all the details that pertain to the plan in your state at **www.savingforcollege.com**.

■ **Educational Savings Account (ESA) or Coverdell Education Savings Account.** It's a savings account to put money aside for college. If you are married and your combined income is less than $150,000 or if you are single and your income is less than $95,000 you can deposit up to $2,000 a year per child. The deposits on this account and the interest they generate are tax exempt as are the withdrawals when you follow the rules. You can save money for elementary, secondary school or for college, but you can't continue to contribute once your child is 18. Also, if your child decides not to attend college, you can't refund the account money to yourself as you can do with a 529 plan. You have to give the funds to your child so you have less control than with a 529 plan.

One More Word about Paying for College

There are many ways to finance your children's college education and credit cards are definitely not the best one. If you don't have any savings, you can't get financial aid and your child doesn't qualify for any scholarships, I suggest that you speak to a financial advisor who can help you come up with a plan to pay for school that will not bankrupt your family. Call your local Chamber of Commerce and ask for the name of a good financial advisor in your area.

Chapter 11

Putting College on the Calendar

We have been talking a lot about all the different activities that you need to do during high school to put your children on the college path. As with many things in this country, timing is everything. Knowing when your teenagers should explore a topic, when they need to prepare for a test, when they should take the test, etc, will ensure a successful outcome. To help you and your kids get organized, here is a calendar that indicates what your child should be doing every month of each one of his or her four years in high school to get to college.

9th Grade

September

Early on, make your expectations about high school known. Discuss with your children their own expectations and concerns. Stress the importance of good grades. Become acquainted with the GPA grading system. Become familiar with the high school's graduation requirements. Ask the guidance counselor about basic academic courses recommended for college bound students. Encourage your child to join extracurricular activities in and out school. Explore special programs—like AVID, The Posse Foundation and A Better Chance—that help Latino students get into the best universities. See Chapter 2 for more information.

October
Contact teachers and ask about your child's progress. Take a trip to the library for information on universities and search college websites. Encourage your child to look through the university pamphlets available in their counselor's office.

November
Encourage your child to volunteer for nonprofit organizations. Volunteering is a valuable experience that instills discipline and responsibility. Community service also enhances a student's college application. Check out Chapter 4 for extracurricular activities and summer programs.

December
Review the first report card and make sure your child is performing appropriately. If not, you can get additional help or ask him or her to request more accelerated classes. College may seem far away, but freshman year grades will be reflected on your kids' transcripts. These grades will carry as much weight as their senior grades will. High school transcripts are as important as the college application.

January
Help your child develop good study habits, especially with midterm exams along the way. Visit websites, such as **www.collegeboard.com**, for more information.

February
Begin making plans for sophomore year. Get your child excited about enrolling in challenging courses that reflect high academic standards.

March
Take a trip to a local college campus. Go by yourselves or take a student-guided tour. Help your children explore their interests, possible careers, and potential universities. Start to identify possible mentors.

April
Attend nearby college fairs. There you will find at least a hundred different college representatives ready to answer any questions you or your child might have. Visit **www.nacacnet.org** for a college fair nearby.

May
With summer approaching, search for a good summer program for your child. Some of them offer financial aid. Turn to Chapter 4 for information on summer programs.

June
Visit websites such as **www.petersons.com** and **www.finaid.org** to evaluate the potential financial cost of your children's college education. Meet with a financial advisor to help you prepare a savings plan for college. Ask about the College Savings Fund 529. Read Chapter 10 for more information.

July

Begin looking into scholarships and loans. See Chapter 10 for information about scholarships. Talk to your children about their career interests and connect with mentors you have identified. Look for more people who are successful in your children's area of interest. You can find mentorship programs at **www.islandnet.com/ ~rcarr/entorprograms.html**. Career assessment tests are also useful in searching for the right major. Check out **www.careerplanner.com**.

August

Encourage your child to spend time with people who are successful in their field of interest to figure out if he or she really likes the field or not. They can visit places of work where they conduct the type of activity he or she likes.

Student to Parent

Rodolfo Vaupel junior, who received a full scholarship from a prestigious university while being on an H4 visa, offers these recommendations for your children in ninth grade:

- When the school doesn't listen to your children, go with them. If you can't go with them, contact a Latin American association or someone else who can go with them to back up their requests.

- Encourage your children to hang out with English speaking individuals—without losing their Latino friends—because that is the only way to truly learn English—by practicing.

- Encourage your children to build a relationship with their teachers and talk to them often.

- Make sure they have good grades starting in 9th grade because every grade counts toward their application for college and scholarships.

- Motivate them to get involved in their school and community, to join clubs and volunteer in organizations. Once they are in a club, encourage them to seek leadership positions within it. Colleges look not only at the clubs students join but at the positions they held.

10th Grade

September
The PSAT (Preliminary Scholastic Assessment Test) exam is right around the corner! This will be a practice run for next year's PSAT which will qualify your child for the National Merit Scholarship. Insist on your child taking practice exams for this PSAT. The PLAN (pre-ACT) is also available in many school districts. Again, explore special programs—like AVID, The Posse Foundation and A Better Chance—that help Latino students get into the best universities. See Chapter 2 for more information.

October
Reiterate the importance of keeping good grades. Also, make sure your child knows not to get discouraged if he or she is having trouble in school. Always seek help from teachers. If necessary, look for extra help.

November
Continue visiting college fairs in your area. Encourage your child to be involved in extracurricular activities and to take on a leadership role.

December
Students should discuss their PSAT results with their guidance counselor, and update their resume file as well.

January
Make a list of universities that your child is interested in. Research the universities to find their location and costs. Encourage your child to connect with students attending those schools to find out first hand what they are like.

February
Ask your child to write or email the admissions office of the universities he is interested in. Request an information packet that includes admission requirements, university history, and tuition costs.

March
Meet with the guidance counselor and discuss your child's eleventh grade year. Ask questions about testing (SAT and ACT), and the upcoming course schedule. Make sure your child is enrolled in college-preparatory courses for his or her upcoming junior year.

April
Register your child for the SAT Subject Tests. The SAT Subject Tests are not required for entrance into all universities, but many do require three of these subject tests to be taken. Your child can register for the SAT Subject Tests, as well as, the SAT at **www.collegeboard.com**.

May

Consider enrolling your children in a college-preparation course for the summer. Encourage your children to volunteer over the summer as well. This is the perfect opportunity for them to expand their college resume. Check out Chapter 4 for summer programs.

June

Your child should begin practice exams for the SAT or ACT. Study together the admissions requirements of the universities he or she is interested in. Many schools require the SAT, while others prefer the ACT. Students can prepare for both tests by using practice exam books or enrolling in test preparation classes. Visit websites such as **www.kaplan.com** and **www.princetonreview.com** for more information.

July

At this time, your child should be receiving mail from many colleges and universities. Make sure he or she reads all the letters or postcards to find if anything interests him or her. Encourage your child to continue to explore areas of interest by spending time with people in those fields or arranging visits to companies, factories, etc. Remember that your child should take advantage of summer programs to develop responsibility, new skills, etc.

August

Students should be receiving their SAT Subject Test results in the mail. Continue to help your children to prepare for the upcoming tests. If your child didn't get involved in a summer program until now, this may be the time to do it.

Inspirational Capsule

For Anna García, an account supervisor for a Public Relations firm in California, there was never a question about attending college. Although she knew it would not be an easy road, she knew she wanted to be an attorney or a journalist. She was the first one in her family to attend college and she is disappointed because her younger siblings do not realize the importance of a higher education. "I wish college would have been a positive experience for me, but it wasn't. It was very hard because I started below par on math and writing and had to take many basic courses," said Anna. With time, she found herself excelling in her undergraduate level writing classes and she knew then that she had something to offer. Although she has a fulltime career, she continues to work toward obtaining her degree in journalism. "I am still working on my degree because I realize the importance and the security that comes along with it. It's taking some time to complete but nevertheless, I will earn my degree," said Anna.

11th Grade

September
Register your child for the PSAT in October. This year it will qualify your child for the National Merit Scholarship.

October
Encourage your child to join extracurricular activities like sports, reading clubs, languages, or volunteering in organizations after school.

November
Plan family trips to visit nearby colleges. Talk about the pros and cons of living far away from home. Encourage your children to follow their dream by attending the best possible school for their career goals.

December
Meet with your child's guidance counselor to discuss the PSAT results. If your child plans to take the ACT, he or she should register in February. Again, insist that your child do practice exams.

January
Prepare for the ACT together. Create flash cards, and find practice exams online or in guide books. Classes are more difficult this year for your child; keep track of your child's academic progress by asking questions about school or contacting the guidance counselor or teacher often.

February
It's time to take the ACT exam. If your child does not do well the first time, he or she should not get discouraged. He or she can take it again at a later date. Keep track of the SAT and ACT registration deadlines. Many juniors take the SAT in May, and a second time in the fall.

March
If your child has decided to take the SAT exam, it's time to prepare. Discuss the course schedule for the upcoming year, and make sure your child is taking challenging classes.

April

Continue reading all college mail, and reply to the colleges that interest your child. Ask the guidance counselor if you should register your child for any SAT Subject Tests.

May

Your child should continue to study for the SAT. Consider SAT preparation courses where they teach children specific skills for this test. Find out about available free courses in your area in organizations such as Let's Get Ready. Go to Chapter 9 for more information.

June

You and your child should visit scholarship and financial aid websites. Decide on all the scholarships that your child should apply for and write on your calendar the deadlines so you don't miss them. Register your child in summer college-preparatory courses, workshops, or internships.

July

Continue visiting colleges, and make plans for fall visits. Take advantage of summer programs that support your child's career goals.

August

Update the final university list. Make a list of the pros and cons for each school. If you don't feel too confident about your ability to help your child through the application process, connect with another family who can do it with you.

<hr>

Inspirational Capsule

Rodolfo Vaupel, Jr. has a good message for you to offer to your children: "Regardless of how worthless education might seem, regardless of how miniscule the chance for you to go to college might be, regardless of how many barriers you might have along the way, DO NOT GIVE UP. Keep trying your hardest to get the best grades possible. If you aim for a C or a B you will fail. If you aim for 100% there is a small chance that you might not get it, but even if you do not get it you will most likely get an A."

<hr>

12th Grade

September
Stress the importance of keeping good grades this year, and taking challenging courses. Colleges will ask for senior grades and credits even after the admissions department has accepted the student.

October
Register your child for the SAT exam offered in January or the ACT in February.

November
Help your child finish applications for scholarships and for college. See Chapter 10 for scholarships. If you are doing this along with another family, participate as much as possible. Showing your support is very important. Remind your child to ask for his or her letters of recommendations.

December

Make sure your child's college applications are sent before the deadline. Gather all the information needed to fill out the FAFSA. See Chapter 10 for FAFSA application.

January

Send the FAFSA to your child's target schools.

February

Encourage your child to check the status of his or her application by consulting the colleges by phone or online. The admissions department will let him or her know if any documents are missing from the application.

March

Encourage your child to keep working hard in school, even though the college application process is over.

April

Once your child has chosen a college or university, make sure you send the deposit by the deadline.

May

Request that the high school sends your child's final transcripts to the college of choice.

June

Encourage your child to take a college-preparatory course in the summer.

July

You and your child should develop a plan for the upcoming year. Discuss courses, jobs, and expectations.

August

If your child is living on campus, have your child contact his or her roommate.

Inspirational Capsule

Ricardo Anzaldúa, who has been for many years a partner at one of the country's most prestigious law firms making a seven-figure salary says, "I'm the chairperson of the Latino Alumni Committee at Harvard Law School Alumni Association. There are a lot of leading Latinos who, like me, have started from a working class background and made a big stride in one generation. There are about 800 Latino alumni of the Harvard Law School, and I would say at least half of them are from working-class backgrounds. That's just one law school of the thousands of professional schools around the country that have been graduating Latinos for generations. Parents need to show their children Latinos who have succeeded so that the kids can see for themselves that they can achieve great things by applying themselves."

Message of Encouragement

Once in a while, we all go through periods when it's hard to remember why we came to the United States. Let me remind you—most of us came in search of a better place to live and raise our children. We came because of the great opportunities to study and to progress that this country offers; because of a freedom we seldom experienced in Latin America and the fact that in this country when you work hard you can fulfill your dreams.

Your job is to help your kids take advantage of all that this country has to offer by supporting their education. The more they study, the better they will do financially and socially. It is through their education that they will occupy positions of leadership that will give them the power to change anything they wish to change to make this a better country and a better world to live in.

About the Author

Mariela Dabbah was born in Buenos Aires, Argentina. She has a Master's Degree in Philosophy and Literature from the University of Buenos Aires. She has lived in New York since 1988, where for twelve years she was one of the owners of an educational book distributor that served the public school system with materials and programs. She developed a Parent Involvement Division that provided teacher and parent training throughout the United States. One of her most exciting and memorable experiences was training Yup'ik parents and librarians in Bethel, Alaska.

Mariela is the award-winning author of *Ayude a sus Hijos a Tener Éxito en la Escuela, Guía para Padres Latinos* (*Help your Children Succeed in School, A Special Guide for Latino Parents*), *Cómo Conseguir Trabajo en los Estados Unidos, Guía Especial para Latinos* (*How to Get a Job in the U.S., A Special Guide for Latinos*), published in Spanish and English, and *The Latino Advantage in the Workplace* (*La Ventaja Latina en el Trabajo*)—also published in both languages and co-authored with

Arturo Poiré—all published by Sphinx Publishing. She has also written *Cuentos de Nuevos Aires y Buena York*, published by Metafrasta.

Mariela is a frequent guest at numerous TV and radio programs such as: "Today in New York" on WNBC, "Exclusiva" on ABC News, "Despierta América" on Univisión, "Cada Día con María Antonieta" on Telemundo, "Negocios Bloomberg" on Bloomberg Radio, "Directo desde Estados Unidos" on CNN En Español, and "All Things Considered" on NPR among others.

As a speaker, Mariela conducts keynotes and workshops at school districts, educational conferences and corporations on the topics of her books. Her mission is to help Latinos navigate the American system. You can find more information about the author on her educational website: **www.marieladabbah.com**.